WISDOM
without
ANSWERS

WISDOM *without* ANSWERS

A Brief Introduction to Philosophy
Fifth Edition

Daniel Kolak

William Paterson University of New Jersey

Raymond Martin

University of Maryland

WADSWORTH
™
THOMSON LEARNING

Australia • Canada • Mexico • Singapore • Spain • United Kingdom • United States

WADSWORTH

THOMSON LEARNING ™

Publisher: Eve Howard
Philosophy Editor: Peter Adams
Assistant Editor: Kara Kindstrom
Editorial Assistant: Chalida
 Anusasananan
Marketing Manager: Dave Garrison

Print/Media Buyer: Rebecca Cross
Permissions Editor: Bob Kauser
Cover Designer: Yvo Riezebos
Compositor: R&S Book Composition
Cover and Text Printer: Webcom

For permission to use material from this
text, contact us by
Web: http://www.thomsonrights.com
Fax: 1-800-730-2215
Phone: 1-800-730-2214

**Library of Congress Cataloging-in-
Publication Data**
Kolak, Daniel.
    Wisdom without answers: a brief
introduction to philosophy/
Daniel Kolak, Raymond Martin.—5th ed.
        p. cm.
    Includes bibliographical references and
index.
    ISBN 0-534-53465-1
    1. Philosophy—Introductions.
I. Martin, Raymond, 1941–   .
II. Title
BD21.K65   2001   2001023777
100—dc21

Wadsworth/Thomson Learning
10 Davis Drive
Belmont, CA 94002-3098
USA

For more information about our products,
contact us: Thomson Learning Academic
Resource Center
1-800-423-0563
http://www.wadsworth.com

International Headquarters
Thomson Learning
International Division
290 Harbor Drive, 2nd Floor
Stamford, CT 06902-7477
USA

UK/Europe/Middle East/South Africa
Thomson Learning
Berkshire House
168-173 High Holborn
London WC1V 7AA
United Kingdom

Asia
Thomson Learning
60 Albert Street, #15-01
Albert Complex
Singapore 189969

Canada
Nelson Thomson Learning
1120 Birchmount Road
Toronto, Ontario M1K 5G4
Canada

To Boonsboro, still nowhere
after all these years

CONTENTS

PREFACE

Socrates was the quintessential philosopher. He knew just this: that, ultimately, he did not know anything. But he had the skill to show others, no matter how sophisticated or erudite or pretentious, that they too knew nothing.

Socrates used philosophy to call *everything* into question, including even what he took for granted in calling everything into question! He used philosophy—as true philosophers always use it—to show us how to pull the rug out from under ourselves, how to cut through the shield of answers that separates us from the mystery.

This book welcomes you to philosophy in the way that Socrates, if he were here, would welcome you: by pulling you out of your answers long enough to experience the wisdom of unknowing.

Many people come to philosophy with the false impression that it is merely a body of knowledge. They expect to receive information rather than to think for themselves. They often assume they know the answers to questions philosophers want to reopen in a fresh way. Thus philosophers often complain that their students are neither motivated nor ready to grapple with the material used in introductory courses.

This book is designed to solve the problems of motivation and preparation. We show, rather than tell, that philosophy is a questioning and reasoning activity, not a body of information. We engage students in the skills they need to interact critically with the material typically presented in an introductory course. Most importantly, we systematically deconstruct students' attachment to ready-made answers, leaving them ready to make new meaning.

For the fifth edition we revised the entire book, making many clarifications and additions. We also updated the essays on further reading in the "Philosophical Connections" section, which can now be found at the back of the book.

We thank all the friends, students, and colleagues who, over the years, have read and commented on drafts and editions, especially Lewis White Beck, Stiv Fleishman, Louis J. Pojman, Susan Leigh Anderson, Mort Winston, Manuel Velasquez, Marshall Missner, Michelle Higginbotham, Richard Hanley, Larry Dobbs, David Reisman, Wendy Zentz, Stephen Bickham, Bruce Jannusch, Leon Miller, David Resnik, Wayne Alt, Stephen Bickham, Michael R. Clifford, and Nancy Hall. We would also thank all the people at Wadsworth for doing such a fine job in the production of the fifth edition.

WISDOM
without
ANSWERS

A Brief Introduction to Philosophy

INTRODUCTION

When we were children we asked questions as children ask them, in complete openness. Where do we come from? What is our purpose in life? What is the nature of the universe in which we live? What happens to us when we die?

We knew we didn't know the answers, and we wanted to know them. We didn't assume the questions were unanswerable or beyond our grasp.

As children we were full of wonder. The world amazed us. As adults we have put away our childish curiosity and live within a structure of answers that silences the fundamental questions that have now lost their power to move us. We found answers, but we lost the mystery. How did this happen?

The problem is not with practical answers. We need them to live successfully. The problem is that each of us, as we shall see, has become dependent on a complex interlocking system of metaphysical answers about self, knowledge, reality, values, and meaning. Often these answers are deeply hidden assumptions so basic to our views of ourselves and the world that it is difficult even to realize we are taking anything for granted. Often they are answers to questions we never even asked. Nevertheless, such metaphysical answers, held in place by our desire for security, end up holding us in place. Locked into our answers, we blind ourselves to the fact that the version of reality we experience and believe in is created as much by ourselves, the observers, as by what we observe.

The problem is not just that we interpret our experience. What, after all, is the alternative? The problem is that we interpret our experience in limiting and rigid ways without even realizing it. We thus create a reality more fixed and stable (and inevitable) than any that actually exists. This seeming solidity may make us feel more secure in our beliefs, but such superficial security rests on answers that

1

ultimately hide as much as they reveal. At best, these answers give us knowledge, not wisdom.

The main obstacle to studying philosophy is not that we don't yet know enough. Far from it. It's that we already know too much. This book is designed to remove this obstacle by welcoming you to philosophy in the way that Socrates, if he were here, would welcome you: by pulling you out of your answers long enough to experience the wisdom of unknowing.

We gain little if we merely replace old answers with new ones. The point is to unravel ourselves completely from dependence on answers, to unsettle what has been settled, and to return to an innocent questioning that leaves all security behind and gets its power not from answers but from the unknown.

Philosophy is an activity, not a body of knowledge. Like all activities, it requires skill. What sort of skill? In a nutshell: the ability to see yourself and the world from many different points of view.

What is a "point of view"? Roughly speaking, a point of view is an interpretation that goes beyond the facts and relies on the assumptions, beliefs, or values of the person making the interpretation. For instance, here's a fact: A three-month-old fetus is intentionally aborted. From one point of view, the abortion was murder. From another point of view, it was not murder. The first point of view relies on the following two assumptions: The fetus was an innocent person, and the intentional killing of innocent persons is murder. The second relies on two different assumptions: The fetus was not a person but, at best, a potential person, and the killing of potential persons is not always murder.

In everyday life, we usually get by perfectly well relying only on our own familiar point of view. But even in daily life, especially in times of conflict, the ability to drop our own point of view and see from another point of view can be extremely helpful. In philosophy this skill is more than just helpful, it is essential. Without it we cannot solve problems that are unsolvable within the confines of our own familiar point of view.

Deep inside, we all know that our own points of view are not the only valid ones. But we tend to push this knowledge to the periphery of our consciousness. This leaves us with an uncomfortable, threatened feeling when we are confronted with points of view antithetical to our own. When we admit that our own points of view are based, ultimately, on questionable assumptions, and we thereby lower our shield against alien points of view, we feel insecure. Most of the time we don't like that feeling. So we allow ourselves to become convinced that our own points of view create the only valid window on the one true reality. Then, when we need to see past the limitations of our own points of view, we get stuck.

The solution, obviously, is to dissolve the glue that binds us to our familiar points of view. Emotional attachment is that glue. To dissolve it, we must first recognize that all of us rely on questionable assumptions much more than we realize. Second, we must set aside our assumptions and learn to see from other points of view. Finally, we need to integrate the insights we gather from these different, and often conflicting, points of view.

Close one eye, and then the other, several times; you will notice a shift between two conflicting, flat perspectives. Open both eyes and the two perspectives become one unified, three-dimensional vision. Integrating insights from our familiar points of view with insight from even one conflicting point of view gives us binocular vision—a sort of "philosophical depth perception"—that can remove the limitations of living and thinking in flatland.

Having a point of view helps us to see ourselves and the world. But if we become too attached to the answers derived from and sustained by our own point of view, we blind ourselves to other points of view. Thus having a point of view can hide as much as it reveals.

Philosophy shows us how to identify the limitations of our own points of view. But it does more: It teaches us how to get outside ourselves—how to cross the barriers of our familiar framework of answers.

* * *

An ancient riddle tells of three wise men from three different empires who showed up one day at the gate to a peaceful kingdom. Each had come to seek asylum from the horrible three-way war that, in spite of all their wise advice, had brought their empires to ruin.

The queen of the peaceful kingdom, herself very wise, arrested the three wise men and brought them in chains before an assembly of her people. With all the citizens present, she asked the three wise men why, if they were so wise, they had not been able to prevent their kingdoms from destroying each other.

"The people of each empire, against the advice of their wise men and their emperors, willed that the other empires be destroyed; the emperors had no choice but to comply," said the first wise man.

"The emperors of each empire, against the advice of their wise men and their people, willed that the other empires be destroyed; the people had no choice but to comply," said the second.

"The wise men of each empire convinced the emperors and the people, against their better judgment, that the other empires must be destroyed; the emperors and the people lacked the wisdom not to comply," said the third.

The queen waited for the murmurs that had suddenly arisen throughout the crowd to subside, and then spoke:

"No one shall be a wise man in my kingdom who does not know why kingdoms collapse. So I ask you three wise men, former enemies, to confer among yourselves and decide which answer is correct. If you cannot reach agreement on that, none of you is fit to be a wise man in my kingdom, and you will all be beheaded for the crimes you have committed against your own people."

The wise men whispered among themselves for several minutes before coming to a conclusion.

"All three answers are correct, your highness," one of them said.

Again there was a murmur through the crowd.

"You are wise indeed," answered the queen, "but I have no place in my kingdom for three clever enemies who might destroy my people the way you have destroyed your own. So I offer you a choice. Either all three of you leave now, together, free and with my blessing to seek your fortunes and asylum elsewhere. Or you stay. But if you choose to stay, two of you must die.

"The rules are simple. I will ask you to solve a riddle that none of my subjects has been able to solve. The one who solves it first will live as the highest of all the wise men in my empire. The other two will die."

Again the three wise men, each of whom was convinced that he was wiser than the other two, and each of whom would have liked to see his two enemies dead, quickly agreed. They chose to stay.

The queen blindfolded the three wise men and then painted a dot on each one's forehead. She asked her citizens to take note of the color of each dot and to keep silent about it. The citizens could see that each dot was red. The queen then took the blindfolds off the three wise men and had them face each other.

"I have painted either a red or a green dot on each of your foreheads," she said loudly to the wise men. "Raise your right hand if you see a red dot on at least one of the foreheads facing you."

Because all three wise men had red dots painted on their foreheads, they each saw that the others had red dots painted on their foreheads and so raised their hands.

"Now," ordered the queen, "without talking, and using only the information provided, you must figure out the color of the dot on your own forehead. The first wise man who can do this and then explain how he did it will live."

The first wise man thought, "The other two have raised their hands. Therefore each of them sees a red dot. I can see that they both have red dots on their own foreheads. But they would both raise their hands whether the dot on my forehead was red or green. So there is no way for me to know whether the dot on my forehead is red or green!"

The second wise man thought, "This riddle is unsolvable. If the dot on my forehead is green, I would see what I am now seeing: the other two with their hands raised, and me with my hand raised. If the dot on my forehead is red, I would also see what I am now seeing: the other two with their hands raised, and me with my hand raised. Because the only information I have to go on is the observation that all three hands are raised, and all three hands would be raised whether the dot on my own forehead is red or green, I have no way of determining whether my dot is red or green."

Ten minutes passed. Suddenly the third wise man exclaimed, "The dot on my forehead is red!" and then explained to the queen and to the stunned crowd how he knew.

How did he do it?

Here's how the third wise man figured out that he, too, had a red dot on his forehead. First, he thought, "There is no way I can figure out the answer by looking merely at what I see from my own point of view. What I see from my point of view would be the same whether my dot was red or green. But the riddle may have an answer. And if it does, and I don't soon discover it, one of the other wise men will, and I shall die. I must, therefore, look for more than what I can now see.

"But what can I look for that I am not now seeing? There are only the three raised hands and the two red dots. If only I could see exactly what Zon and Hsu, the other two wise men, are seeing from their points of view! Perhaps I can. How do things look to them?

"Zon has a red dot, but he doesn't know it. What he does know is that Hsu has a red dot and that I, Sol, have whatever color dot I have. Suppose, then, that I have a red dot. Then Zon would be in the same predicament I'm now in, namely that of seeing two red dots, and so could not solve the riddle.

"Suppose, then, that I have a green dot. In that case Zon sees that I have a green dot and that Hsu has a red dot. But if I have a green dot and Hsu has a red dot, Zon would *eventually* be able to figure out that he too has a red dot, for Zon would reason as follows: 'Sol has a green dot, and Hsu has raised his hand, indicating that he sees at least one red dot; because Sol has a green dot, the red dot that Hsu sees must belong to me (Zon). Hence, I (Zon) have a red dot.'

"Hsu also has a red dot but doesn't know it. What he does know is that Zon has a red dot and that I—Sol—have whatever color dot I have. Hence, Hsu is in exactly the same predicament as Zon. Hence, if I had a green dot, Hsu would *eventually* be able to figure out that he too has a red dot.

"But because ten minutes have elapsed, and neither Zon nor Hsu has figured out that he has a red dot, I too must have a red dot!"

At this point Sol informed the queen that he had a red dot, explaining that he came to that conclusion by looking at the situation from the points of view of the others.

The story ends with the beheading of Zon and Hsu and the proclamation by the queen that Sol was now the wisest man in the kingdom. She put special emphasis on the word *man*, and everyone laughed. She then honored Sol by naming the sun after him and offering him any of the royal jewels he most favored.

Sol thanked her but asked to be given instead the little brush and the can of red paint. He then walked among the crowd and continued on throughout the kingdom, painting red dots on all the people's foreheads as a reminder of what had happened that day.

This all happened a long, long time ago, in a land far, far away, and so, of course, most people have forgotten about it. They have also forgotten the lesson that learning to see ourselves and the world from different points of view can sometimes keep us from losing our heads. Perhaps you too will forget. But one day soon you are bound to come across someone with a red dot painted on his or her forehead. And then you will remember.

WHERE

Where are you?

Obvious answer: "Here."

Where is "here"?

If you were "here" with us, you would be in Boonsboro. Some of our friends say Boonsboro is nowhere. The map says it's a small town in western Maryland. Maryland is somewhere—on the east coast of the United States. It might be in the Northern Hemisphere. Or it might be in the Western Hemisphere. Or perhaps both. We're not sure. It doesn't really matter. What hemisphere we're in depends upon an arbitrary partitioning of the Earth.

Where is Earth? For if we know we're on Earth but we don't know where Earth is, we don't really know where we are. Fortunately, another map tells us Earth is the third planet from the sun in our solar system.

Where is our solar system? A larger map tells us our solar system is in an outer arm of the Milky Way galaxy, which is in the Local Cluster of galaxies, which, finally, is in the universe. But where is the universe?

Now there's a question: *Where is the universe?*

We're out of maps. You might think the universe is everywhere. But this answer at most locates us *within* the universe. It does not give the universe a location. Suppose you are lost at sea and over the radio a distant voice asks where the sea is. Looking around, you say, "Everywhere." This merely locates you somewhere on the sea. It does not locate the sea. Unless you know what lies beyond the borders of the sea, you are still lost.

So, what lies beyond the borders of the universe? Space? No, the universe can't be *in* space, because by *universe* we mean the totality of everything. All space must be in the universe. Where, then, is the universe?

Up to now we've determined the position of each thing by locating it within a containing space. The universe, however, is the ultimate containing space: By definition, the universe contains *everything*. The universe could be somewhere only if there were something the universe did not contain. But there isn't. The universe, therefore, is not anywhere at all; it's nowhere.

So, right now we're in a universe that is nowhere! In one sense, of course, we're still somewhere. For instance, as we write this we are in Boonsboro, Maryland, on the east coast of the United States, in the Northern or Western Hemisphere, on the planet Earth, in our solar system, inside an outer arm of the Milky Way galaxy, in the Local Cluster of galaxies, inside the universe. But, ultimately, *we're all nowhere.*

What seems so solidly in place all around us is floating freely in nothing. Ultimately, there is absolutely no support, no foundation, no container, *nothing* to make the whole secure.

Does that make us feel insecure? You bet it does. Perhaps that's partly why we've partitioned the universe not just into galaxies and solar systems and planets and hemispheres and countries and cities, but even down to streets and numbered houses. We can locate each other. But we cannot locate the whole. We're all still nowhere.

Suppose you're on an oceanliner. You hear a voice over the intercom: "This is the captain speaking. I have no idea where we are. We're completely lost." Your friend says, "Is the captain crazy? He may be lost. The ship may be lost. But I'm not lost. I'm on deck 3, cabin 381. I know exactly where I am."

Your friend's answer might serve some practical purposes. He might want to have his tuxedo pressed for the evening ball. But his answer is also a way of shielding himself from the truth that everyone aboard the ship is lost.

So, where are we? Above us there's a sky full of stars. Below us the Earth. Behind us a mountain. In front, a long meadow descends into a valley. Woods to the right and left. We *know* where we are. We're exactly where some of our friends say we are: nowhere.

Where are you?

WHEN

2

Here you are, *now*, in the present. When is that? When is the present?

Obvious answer: "Now." But when is "now"?

For us, as we are writing this, it is 9:49 P.M., Eastern Standard Time, Friday, January 5, 1990. We all know when 1990 is: It is the first year in the last decade of the twentieth century, at the tail end of a conventionally demarcated one hundred years, fifty (or so) centuries after the beginning of civilization. When, though, are these centuries?

These fifty centuries of history are a small time segment within the approximately fifteen-billion-year time span that is currently the best estimate of the age of the universe. To comprehend such awesome lengths of time, let us compress the entire fifteen billion years of the universe's existence into one calendar year so that each second corresponds to 475 years, each month represents more than one billion years, and the entire 365 days equals the present age of the universe.

Using this scale, on January 1 the universe "begins." Not until well into the universe's spring, in May, does cosmic debris coalesce, due to gravity, into our local galaxy of stars—the Milky Way. By the end of summer, four months later, our solar system forms out of gaseous remnants while the sun, a seventh-generation star, begins to shine. About one week later, in mid-September, the planetary fireballs cool and become the planets, among them Earth. Another week or so later, in early fall, Earth spawns primitive life in its primordial waters. Not until just before winter, in mid-December, do complex organisms such as fish, land plants, and insects emerge. By the time winter returns in the third week of December, amphibians, reptiles, and trees have appeared, followed a few days later by the first dinosaurs. The dinosaurs last three days. As the great reptiles are becoming extinct, the first mammals arrive. On December 30, primates begin to populate Earth.

It is December 31, New Year's Eve, the last day of the cosmic year. Two hours before midnight, at 10:00 P.M., humanoids evolve; at 11:40 P.M., *Homo erectus,* the first primate to walk on two legs; ten minutes later, *Homo sapiens;* at 11:57 P.M., Neanderthals; a minute and a half later, Cro-Magnons. Finally, at 11:58 and 57 seconds, just one minute and three seconds before the present moment, modern humans—*Homo sapiens sapiens*—awaken to find themselves not merely existing but also contemplating their existence.

One minute later, at 11:59 and 55 seconds, philosophy and science are born. Then, for five fleeting seconds, the rest of history up to the present moment unfolds.

On the cosmic scale, your entire life—provided you live to a ripe old age—will last almost (but not quite) two-tenths of one second.

So, here you are right now, in the present, locating yourself temporally at one end of the fifteen billion years through which the universe has existed. But what about that entire fifteen-billion-year span within which all time is located? When is that? In other words, when does the totality of the time that is the duration of the universe occur? *When* does the universe exist?

When *could* it exist? The universe contains not just all of space but also all of time. Just as there is no space outside the universe, so also there is no time.

When does the universe happen? Surprisingly, never. *The universe, which is nowhere, never happens.*

But what about now, what about *right now?* This present moment, when is that? When does it happen? Ultimately, never. Locally, however, we can assign it a temporal point. For instance, now, as we are writing this, it is 1:11 A.M., Saturday, January 6, 1990. When, though, are you reading this? Isn't the present moment in which you are reading this also a now for you? Isn't it *your* now?

You look at your watch, just as we did. You "see the time." You check the calendar, or your memory, and note the date. You think, "It is no longer 1:11 A.M., January 6, 1990." For you! But for us? Here we are. It is January 6. Our clock says 1:15 already. As we write this, you, the (future) reader (unless you are not yet born) are right now (on January 6, 1990) somewhere probably miles away, perhaps asleep, and you have no idea, at this time (at 1:15 on January 6, 1990), that you will someday (in our future) read this. But you *will* read this. You *are* reading this! Yet, from the perspective of *our* present, the chapter you are now reading is not yet completed. As far as we are concerned, you are not somewhere over there, in the future, reading. You are somewhere over here, in the present, perhaps sleeping.

So, where are you? Are you in our future (your present), reading, or in our present (your past), sleeping? And where are we? Are we there with you in our future, perhaps teaching, or are we here, as we think we are, in our present, writing? Wherever any of us are, we never find ourselves in the future or in the past but only in the present. For you and for us too the events we experience are going on *now*, in "the present." Yet these different events—your reading and our writing—occur at *different* nows.

We think that our now is really happening and your now has not yet happened. You think that your now is really happening and our now is no longer happening. Who is right? *Which now—yours or ours—is the one actually going on?* Which now is the *real* now?

Ordinary experience suggests a commonsense view about the relation between time and reality: Whatever is going on now is real, and everything real (or fully real) is going on now. You are now having the experience of reading a book. That experience and the book are both real. Even if you were hallucinating, your experience would be real—a real hallucinatory experience. If the book were not really there, still your hallucinatory experience of seeming to see the book would be there. Compare, say, a hallucinatory experience (that someone actually had) of a chair with a merely possible experience (that no one actually had) of a chair. The actual hallucinatory experience, even though hallucinatory, is part of the real world. A merely possible experience (that no one actually had) is not part of the real world (even if it were a possible experience of a real object).

Part of the commonsense view is that anything not in the present is unreal, or at least less real, than whatever exists in the present. The past, we tend to think, is "gone," not merely because past events are not present events but because past events no longer exist—either at the present moment or at any moment. Past events (such as, from your present point of view, our writing this), although they once existed, do not exist in the present and hence are no longer real.

So, according to the commonsense view of the relation between time and reality, if you remember something you did as a child, the events you remember no longer exist and hence are now unreal (or less real) than your current memory experience of those events. Your current experience, even if a memory experience, exists in the present and hence is real. Similarly with the future. If you know now that to-morrow you will reread this chapter, the event of your rereading it tomorrow is not real until it happens. Until an event happens it is only a mere possibility, not an actuality. And then once the event has happened it vanishes into the past and hence, once again, is not real. In sum, according to common sense, reality resides in the present; past events and future events, since they are not in the present, are not real.

In that case, right now, as you are reading these words, our present experience of writing them is no longer real. And from our present point of view, your experience of reading this is not yet real. Similarly, from the point of view of some future time at which, for instance, you are lying on your deathbed horrified at the thought of your life ending forever, your present experience of reading these words is no longer real. It has been extinguished with the past, just as you (lying on your deathbed) are about to be extinguished.

Of course, you say to yourself, "But I am not lying on my deathbed now. I am now reading a book." But when you will be lying on your deathbed, you will not say, "There I am now, reading a book." You will say, "Here I am now, dying."

When does your death take place? From your present point of view, sometime in the future. From your point of view at the moment of death, your death is happening now. Similarly, from your present point of view, your birth happened in the past. On the other hand, from your mother's point of view at the moment of your birth, your birth is happening now.

But right now, as you are reading this, probably you believe that neither the event of your death nor the event of your birth is as real as the present moment. Your birth is over with. Your death has not yet happened. *Now* there are for you only present events such as your reading this. Because you are reading these words, you are alive. Your life—not your death—is what you think is real. But if the moments in which you were born and in which you will die are real—just as real as right now (even though those moments are in your past and your future)—then there is a sense (perhaps a profound one) in which even now, as you stare at this page, you are not yet born and you are already dead.

If you are there, in the past, being born, and in the future, dying, then your birth and death and the circumstances surrounding them are somehow fixed. Time, then, would be like a reel of motion picture film, with all moments fully there, all equally real. Each moment, each present, like the individual frames of a movie, is projected so as to give the illusion of the flow of time. At any one frame (at any one moment) the apparent flow is from what you regard as your past to what within that same frame (within that same moment) you regard as your future. The reel of film, however, already contains all the frames, all the moments, not just of your life but of all lives, and the apparent flow from past to present to future is but a rapidly flickering illusion.

From within the commonsense view it is difficult to see how all nows might be equally real. Yet, if we pause to think about it, the commonsense view becomes deeply suspect. At each different moment (at each different now) we feel certain that the now of that moment is the only real one. This feeling of certainty seems to arise not for any good reason but, rather, merely because we always find ourselves looking outward at all other moments, past and future, from the limited and limiting point of view of a particular now. Viewing ourselves from the perspective of a particular moment blinds us to the genuine possibility that every moment may—at that and every other moment—be equally real.

Suppose we adopt a point of view that abstracts away from our feeling of being located at only one particular moment, at one single now. We might then be able to break the spell of the feeling that binds us to the commonsense view. For instance, suppose you could see the history of the entire universe spread before you all at once. What would it look like?

Imagine all the events of the universe spread out like a roll of motion picture film unwound from the reel, left to right, placed flat against a uniform field of light. Gazing down from above along the individual frames, you find the event of your birth. Somewhere to the right there is your death, a snapshot moment captured forever in a still frame within the cosmic film. To the left of your birth, dinosaurs graze. To the right of your death, the sun explodes. The sequence of frames (moments) in which we write this (January 5 and 6, 1990) lies to the left of (before) the sequence of frames in which you read this.

From such a bird's-eye view of the universe, what could make it seem that any particular now is any more real than any other? Nothing. Nor would the notions of past, present, and future have the significance common sense accords to them. Ordinarily, by the past we mean everything before the present; by the present, everything right now; and by the future, everything after the present. From the timeless perspective, however, there would be no privileged "present" moment relative to which we could demarcate the past from the future. All moments—from the beginning to the end of time—would be there, spread out in eternity, equally present, equally now, equally real.

Which, then, is the real now—ours as we write this or yours as you read this? Or are all nows equally real (or, perhaps, equally unreal)?

As we write these words it is 5:43 A.M. Eastern Standard Time, Saturday, January 6, 1990. From our point of view, this is now. From your point of view, this (our present now) is then. But from the point of view of the universe as a whole, this now—like your now, like all nows—is nowhere, always, and never.

WHO

3

Who are you?

When someone asks who you are, the obvious answer—your name—pops into your head. You don't have to think about it. But your name is only a word. Your name isn't who you are. The *you* in "Who are you?" doesn't refer to a word. It refers to *you*.

Who, then, are you?

Besides your name, there are your interests, your job, where you live, and so on. But these also are not essential to who you are. You can change your interests or your job or where you live without changing your identity. *You* does not refer to your interests, your job, or where you live. So, again, who are you?

There is your age, who your parents are, all the various things you did from the time you were born until the present moment, what you're like as a person right now, and so on. To which of these, if any, does *you* refer?

What began as a simple request has turned into a complex puzzle. You can't know who you are unless you know to what *you* refers. The obviousness and seeming simplicity of the question "Who are you?" only masks the fact that the reference of *you* is unknown. So let's begin with a question that refers to you and that you can answer. From the answer you may be able to determine the reference of *you*.

One of the most obvious things you think you know about yourself is your age. So, how old are you?

This time, instead of a name, a number popped into your head almost instantaneously. You didn't have to think about it.

The question "How old are you?" is obviously about you. And you think you know the answer. So to what does *you* in "How old are you?" refer? The answer that popped into your head was the age of your body. So perhaps *you* refers to your body.

Your body may be a valid reference of *you*. This conventional reference serves well for many practical purposes. But it is not the only possible reference. For instance, there is the "soul theory," according to which *you* refers to an immaterial soul, in which case you could be millions of years old or even infinitely old. And we've all heard the "you're only as old as you feel" story; if *you* refers to how old you feel psychologically or emotionally, or intellectually, then you might be either younger or older than your body. Your body may be old, your mind young. Perhaps there's a child in you. Perhaps you're only sixteen. Or ten. Or even younger.

Of course, all of us easily recognize that these alternative numbers rest on theories and stories. Thus, when asked our ages, we don't think of any of these alternative numbers. Instead, we automatically give an answer that we assume is a hard fact. We tend to forget that the standard number—the number generated by the hidden assumption that you are the age of your body—also rests on a theory. Like every theory, the standard way of interpreting our ages includes some assumptions—in this case, one of the assumptions is that the bodies we have now are the same bodies we were born with.

Look at a picture of yourself as a baby and then look in a mirror. The face in the mirror and the face in the photograph—including the eyes doing the seeing—haven't a single cell in common. The standard way of determining our ages requires us to assume that we are the ages of our bodies and that we have the same bodies throughout our lives. This assumption masks the impermanence of the stuff of which we're made.

We don't mean these assumptions are false (though we allow for that). Rather, we mean, first, that the assumptions are interpretations that go well beyond the data available to experience and, second, that they go beyond the data in such a way that some underlying truth—in this case, the impermanence of the physical constituents of which our bodies are composed—is masked. The masking occurs because these assumption-laden interpretations become so familiar that eventually they generate a feeling of obviousness. This feeling of obviousness then actually alters the way we experience the world. Before we know it, we forget that our experience is always colored (sometimes distorted) by our interpretations.

Imagine, for instance, that you're about to go swimming in the Mississippi River. You remember swimming in it as a child. You might assume without question that the river you are about to swim in is the same river you swam in as a child. But the river is made of water, and the water is always changing. Hence the famous aphorism "You can't step into the same river twice." In one sense the river you swam in as a child no longer exists. All rivers are new. Although we may say that the Mississippi is the same river from day to day, we can all easily recognize that *same* is just a label, *Mississippi* just a name. We know that to get to the truth we have to look beyond labels and names to the actual thing. Naming a river "the Mississippi" and then saying that it is "the same river" from day to day doesn't *make* it the same river, except in a trivial, merely verbal sense. Though we're accustomed to thinking of the Mississippi as the same river from day to day, we're really accepting a convenient theory, one that obscures the fact that the reference of the word *Mississippi* is ambiguous. The word could refer to the water, the river bank, or possibly something else.

The grammatical structure of the question "Can you step into the same river twice?" is subject-verb-object. The river is the object. We focus on the object and take the subject for granted because we are the subject and we have been conditioned to take for granted that our identities extend for the durations of our lives. Our own persistence, even more than the persistence of the river, is cloaked in obviousness. So we don't easily see that there are two reasons for thinking that you can't step into the same river twice. The first, obvious one, has to do with the object in question: the river. It leaves *you* completely out of the picture. The second, subtle one, has to do with the subject: you. It puts *you* into the picture. The first reveals the impermanence of the stuff of which the river is made. The second reveals the impermanence of the stuff of which you are made.

If *same river* refers to the physical parts of which the river is made—the "same water"—the Mississippi of today is not the Mississippi of a few years ago. But to what does the *you* refer when we talk about "the same you"? If it refers to the physical parts of which you are made, then, like the river, the *you* of today is not the *you* of a few years ago.

The Mississippi is made mostly of water. It completely replaces almost all its water every seven weeks. You are made mostly of cells, each of which is mostly water. You completely replace almost all your cells every seven years. Millions of your cells have been replaced since you began reading this chapter. And as you are reading right now, your atoms are a constant whirlpool of dizzying motion so tumultuous that when you try to look closely at the atoms themselves, the parts of which they are made bubble away from you. You can no more grasp them than you can grasp a handful of water.

Like a river, you too are made mostly of water that is constantly being replaced. But you believe that you, unlike a river, are a continuously existing entity—you are someone with an identity that extends over time. Who?

Again, there is your name. But rivers have names, too. Your name can't be who you are. Your name is only another way of referring to *you*. So who are you, really? We turned to the question of your age to find the reference of *you*. Suppose *you* refers to the actual physical constituents of your present body. The average age of those constituents is no more than seven years. Only your neurons are older. So if you are the age of the constituents of your body, you are no more than seven years old!

Most of your neurons are older than seven years. The constituents out of which your neurons are composed, however—ions, electrons, and so on—are in constant flux. And, in any case, *you* does not refer to your individual neurons. First, if *you* referred to your individual neurons, "How are you today?" would be a question about how your individual neurons are doing. But it isn't. Individual neurons have properties like being long or short, firing or not firing, and so on—not properties like being happy or depressed. The question "How are you today?" is a question about how *you* are doing. The only reason neurons are even worth discussing is that they are a part of your body that has something to do with your mind. If it turned out that your liver retained the same cells over the years, we would not think that *you* refers only to your liver.

Second, to suppose that *you* refers to your *collection* of neurons—your brain—raises the question of whether the brain matters to the preservation of your identity. It seems that you could survive the replacement of all your neurons with exact replicas. Consider an analogy. A friend lends you his copy of Beethoven's Fifth Symphony recorded on cassette tape. Using professional recording equipment, you make a qualitatively identical copy of that sound structure onto an exactly similar tape. What matters to the preservation of the recorded performance of Beethoven's Fifth Symphony is the music (the sound structure), not the tape on which the music is recorded. Suppose that in the process of transferring the music you accidentally destroy the original tape, and so you give your friend the qualitatively identical tape with the newly recorded music on it. If your friend claims that you destroyed the recorded performance of Beethoven's Fifth Symphony that he lent you, clearly he would be mistaken. You merely destroyed the tape on which that performance was recorded. The recorded performance has been perfectly preserved on the new tape.

If the analogy between people and sound structures is a good one, then what makes you *you* is not neurons—the brain—but, rather, the psychological information encoded on the neurons. Consider, for instance, science fiction dramas in which the entire pattern of someone's brain and body is beamed via a teletransporter from a spaceship (where the original atoms are destroyed) to a planet's surface where the exact pattern of the person's entire physical and mental structure is embedded in different, but qualitatively similar, atoms. Suppose you underwent such a procedure. Would you regard it as a way of continuing to exist or of dying and being replaced by a replica? We can even imagine the teletransporter instantaneously beaming you to the place where you're already at: in effect, instantaneously switching each and every one of your atoms with an exactly similar atom so that no one—not even you—could tell whether any change had occurred.

Such examples suggest that what matters most to the preservation of your identity is not your atoms (not even your neurons) but, rather, the patterns of information encoded on your atoms. It is as if the brain is like a cassette tape on which your personal identity is recorded. Or perhaps a better analogy (one that includes the active, not just passive, functioning of your mind) would be to think of your brain as being like the hardware of an extremely powerful and complex computer onto which your mind (your personality, thought patterns, memories, and so on)—the software—is encoded. Provided the process is accurate, software can travel from one computer to another without loss of identity.

Perhaps, then, *you* refers to your mind. However, just as your body is not one seamless whole, so your mind is not one seamless whole. Your body is made up of physical parts. Your mind is made up of "mental parts." These "mental parts" are individual mental states: sensations, emotions, and thoughts. If you are the age of your mental states, then how old are you? How old are your sensations, emotions, and thoughts? Perhaps they are the same age as the automatic number you think of when you think of your age. But are they?

Look again at that childhood photograph of yourself. Not a single atom of a single cell you see in the photograph is still there. The hand holding the photograph and the hand in the photograph haven't a single cell in common. Now ask yourself whether the person in the photograph and the person looking at the photograph have a single sensation, emotion, or thought in common.

Do you remember the sensations, emotions, and thoughts going on when the photograph was taken? Do you remember who took the photograph, where you came from to get in front of the camera, where you went after the shutter clicked, and so on? Probably you don't remember many of these things. Just as you once may have believed that your present body and the body in your childhood photograph are one and the same, so also you may believe that your present mind and your mind when the photograph was taken are one and the same. But your sensations, emotions, and thoughts have changed even more drastically than your physical parts. What then makes you believe that you are the same person as the one in the photograph?

If *you* refers to your mind, how old are you? Well, how old are your mental states—your sensations, emotions, and thoughts?

If you're sitting down, focus on the sensation of the pressure of your rear against the chair. That sensation is a mental state. Here are some others: the sensation of breath passing through your nostrils and into your lungs; the sensation of muscular tension in your fingers and arms as you hold this book; the feeling of anticipation (where is this paragraph leading?) and of yearning (your desire for completion); the changing sensations as you move your body; various memories of things you've experienced; and so on.

All the sensations, emotions, and thoughts you are now experiencing exist in the present. Even your recalling a memory, which is *of* the past, isn't itself *in* the past. Memories can be experiences only in the present, consisting of sensations, emotions, and thoughts. So, how old are your current sensations, emotions, and thoughts?

Focus on the conscious sensation of the pressure of your rear against the chair. How old is that sensation? Has it been there as long as you have been physically sitting in your chair? No. If you pay close attention, you will see that the actual conscious sensation of pressure is only (at most) seconds old. Remember that we're not talking about the underlying physical basis for your sensation of pressure. (We have already considered the physical parts of your body.)

We're asking about the actual conscious sensation of pressure itself. It is at most seconds old.

What about your other conscious mental states—how old are they? They too are (at most) seconds old. Just as the face you now see in the mirror and the face in the childhood photograph are composed of qualitatively similar yet different cells, so also the mind looking at the photograph and the mind that was there when the photograph was taken are composed of qualitatively similar yet different sensations, emotions, and thoughts. You may remember having sensations, emotions, and thoughts similar to those you now have. But those past sensations, emotions, and thoughts are not your present sensations, emotions, and thoughts. For instance, suppose that three years ago you sat on the very same chair sensing the pressure of the seat. You now remember this. That previous sensation of pressure is not the one going on right now. The present sensation—the one that now exists—is (at most) seconds old.

What about your memory of that previous sensation? How old is it? The sensation you remember of sitting in the chair happened three years ago. That is what people mean when they say a memory is an old one. But, like all your other sensations, emotions, and thoughts, your experience of remembering is (at most) seconds old. Your remembering started as you were reading the sixth or seventh sentence of the previous paragraph. It will last (at most) until your attention moves on to something else. Any subsequent remembering of the sensation of sitting in this chair three years ago will not be *this* remembering. It will be a new remembering. This present remembering—the one going on right now—like all your other sensations, emotions, and thoughts is itself (at most) seconds old.

So, how old are you? If *you* refers to your mind—that is, to your present conscious mental states—then you are (at most) a few seconds old.

Our standard theory about our ages may have great practical value. But the standard theory misleads us: It makes our persistence and our solidity seem to extend beyond our theories. In doing so, it makes *us* seem to extend beyond our theories. That's why our ages seem like facts carved in stone instead of part of a theory. Yet we accept the standard theory without question as absolute truth. Why? And who, or what, does the accepting? Who are you?

The question is ambiguous. It isn't clear what *you* refers to. *You* might refer to your physical parts or to your mental states. In either

case, the foundation for your belief about who you are—that, whoever you are, you are the same person from day to day—is questionable. Just as there is no such thing as a permanent river, except in
theory, so also there is no such thing as a permanent person, except
in theory. Just as all rivers are always brand new, except in theory, so
also all people are always brand new—except in theory.

Our theories may or may not be true. But if we don't have good
reason for believing them to be true, then (unless perhaps we are
somehow reliably plugged into the truth in a way that automatically
turns our beliefs into knowledge) even if we believe our theories and
they do turn out to be true, we don't know they are true. And in that
case we don't know who we are.

Note that your mental states change much more quickly than
does the physical stuff of which you are made. Hence, claiming that
you refers to physical stuff is analogous to claiming that it's not the
water but the riverbanks that make rivers the same from day to day
and year to year. The water constantly changes but the riverbanks remain relatively constant. But even riverbanks flow, just like rivers,
only more slowly.

If it doesn't seem obvious that even riverbanks flow, take a ride
on the Mississippi. Don't get off too soon. Go all the way to the end.
The waters of the Mississippi empty into the Gulf of Mexico. The
banks of the Mississippi empty into the Mississippi Delta. The riverbanks your ancestors may have walked on are now part of the Delta.

When you're visiting the Delta, find a conch shell. Go to a quiet
spot and hold the shell to your ear; you will hear what sounds like
flowing water. People call it the sound of the ocean, but really it's
only the echo of blood flowing through your ear canal. It's the sound
of you. It's the sound of a river.

FREEDOM

Why are you reading this?

Because you want to. Even if somebody told you to read it, it would make no difference: If you didn't want to do what you were told, you wouldn't be reading this. But you are reading this. So whether you simply want to read this or were told to read this and now are reading it because you want to do what you were told, either way you are doing what you want. But in reading this are you acting *freely?* That is, is it up to you whether you are reading this?

The answer may seem obvious. You're doing what you want. Therefore, you're doing it freely. But is what you want up to you? When you're doing what you want, are *you* in control—do you control your wants—or do your wants control you?

Suppose you got orders to read this. You find yourself obeying them. Then you get orders to question the orders. So you question them. Then you get orders to stop questioning. So you stop. You'd quickly realize that you have no freedom, that you are under the control of the orders. An order is a command, usually verbal. But suppose the orders came not as verbal commands but as direct urges to do so-and-so.

Being controlled by urges would be more subtle than being controlled by verbal commands because you could easily take the urges to be under your own control. You could pretend they were up to you. You could even call them *wants*. When you felt the urge to do X, you could say to yourself, "I want to do X." You could thus cleverly hide from yourself the fact that whatever is pulling your strings (either some internal program to which you have no direct access or some external programmer) is hidden by your having wants instead of orders. To get you to read this, in other words, the program (or programmer) sends the want—a nonverbal command—as a way of pulling your strings without your directly sensing it. In that case, is what you want up to you? Would you be free? It would seem not. You would have at most only the illusion of freedom. Your doing what you want would mask the fact that your wants would be controlling you, not you them.

Aren't you in exactly this situation? You don't *make* your wants, you just have them. They arrive into your consciousness, triggering various behaviors. For instance, if you are hungry now you may want to eat. Surely you did not freely choose to want to eat. People do not choose to want to eat but merely discover by paying attention to their experiences of hunger that they want to eat. But if we do not choose our wants and our wants determine our choices and our choices determine our actions, then, ultimately, our actions are not up to us and hence, it would seem, we do not perform them freely. So even if right now in reading this you are doing what you want, because your wants are not up to you, your reading this is not up to you either and, thus, it would seem, you are not reading this freely.

Suppose, though, that you both want and don't want to do something—say, you want to eat chocolate and you also want not to eat it, that is, you want to resist your desire to eat it. Which do you do? Well, which want is stronger? You will act—*must* act—according to your stronger want. So your behavior—whatever you wind up doing—will be just a product of one want's superseding another. For instance, suppose you want chocolate because it tastes so good and you want not to eat it—or even to want it—because you believe that eating it is bad for you. You can't help but want chocolate now. That you want it now is not something you choose but something you simply discover about yourself. You can, perhaps, condition yourself—say, by enrolling in a chocolate-abuser's therapy program—so that in the future you will no longer want chocolate. Suppose you do that and that somewhere down the road you lose your desire for chocolate. In that case, is what you want in the future up to you?

It all depends. How did your present desire to want to stop eating chocolate—and hence your desire to condition yourself to stop wanting it—come about? Perhaps you read a report that chocolate is bad for you and your reading the report made you want to stop wanting chocolate. But how did that second want—wanting to stop wanting chocolate—come about? Was it something you chose or something you merely discovered had happened within you on the basis of having read that report? Surely the latter. It isn't up to you how you feel about such a report. You don't choose your feelings.

You just find yourself feeling however you feel. Thus, even if you condition yourself to feel differently in the future or otherwise alter your circumstances so that some want you now have but do not want to have does not arise, your urge now to condition yourself or alter your circumstances is something you discover about yourself; it is not something you choose.

Ultimately, then, wantings and not-wantings are both things that happen to us, not things we choose. It is not up to us what we want or don't want. Thus even our so-called uncoerced choices—that is, the ones that are not coerced from the outside—are coerced from the inside. These so-called uncoerced choices are ultimately no more up to us than are the choices we make in response to external coercion. The only difference is that we can easily notice the external coercion as such whereas the internal coercion is not so readily apparent. Our freedom, then, would seem to be an illusion. How could even your reading this right now be a free action, regardless of how you came to read it? How could anything any of us ever does be free?

Perhaps, in suggesting that an action is free only if *ultimately* it is up to you whether you do it, we have set the standards for freedom too high. Why can't we lower our standards and say simply that you acted freely provided your action was a consequence of your choice and your choice came about in a normal way, uncoerced by any external agency? For instance, why can't we say that your act of reading this now is free if you are reading it merely because you want to? Well, of course, we—you—can *say* that. That is the way we ordinarily conceive of freedom, and you can, if you like, stick to that ordinary conception. It's up to you, even if it's not ultimately up to you. Yet choosing to speak one way rather than another, which is a merely verbal matter, would not erase the fact that your choices and behavior would be up to you only in a watered-down way. That is, it would not erase the fact that a free act of this sort might nevertheless be caused by conditions over which no one, and certainly not you, ultimately has any control. With such a conception of freedom you would not ultimately be in any more control of your so-called free choices and behaviors than are the cells in your body in control of whether they divide or are rivers in control of whether they flow downhill.

If you still think you have freedom in some more robust sense than this, then ask yourself: If you are free, when did you first become free? For if you are free now, then there must have been some first free action. Surely you were not born free. When you were first born you reacted to your environment in basically preprogrammed ways. Just as you did not choose to have two eyes, a nose, a brain (with all its structures), each of your limbs, and so on—none of which was up to you—so also you did not choose how to react to light, heat, hunger, pain, or even the smiling face of your mother. We all start life without any freedom. Thus our actions now cannot possibly be free unless there was some first free action that we performed sometime after we were born. When was *your* first free action? If you never could have performed a first free action, then you couldn't have performed a second free action, or a third, and so on, up to and including your current action of reading these words.

Suppose, then, for the sake of argument, that you performed your first free action at your fifth birthday party when you punched your little brother in the nose. (As we shall see, it doesn't matter whether you think your first free action occurred earlier or later than when you were five—exactly the same issues arise.) *Could* this action of yours—your hitting your brother—have been free? Only if the reasons for which you hit him, or the circumstances in which you hit him, made it free. Could there have been any such reasons or circumstances?

Suppose you hit your brother because you chose to hit him and you chose to hit him because you wanted to hit him. In that case, we have to ask, *Why* did you want to hit him? However complicated the details, only two types of things could have caused you to want to hit your brother. One of these was your external environment just prior to your hitting him: Say, your brother was standing in front of you, pointing his finger at you, sticking his tongue out, your parents were nowhere in sight, and so on. The other was your internal environment just prior to your hitting him: You were angry at your brother, you were disposed to act on that anger, you had other relevant wants and aversions, and so on.

But if this is what caused you to hit your brother, then because you did not freely choose any aspect of either your external or your internal environment, you did not freely choose to hit your brother. We know you did not freely choose any aspect of either your external or your internal environment because we have been supposing, for the sake of argument, that if your hitting your brother was done freely, then it was your first free action. Since a free choice is itself a free action, your freely choosing any aspect of your external or internal environment would have been a free action of yours that occurred before your first free action, which, of course, is impossible.

So, if your hitting your brother was completely the result of your external and internal environments just before you hit him and you did not freely choose any aspect of your external or internal environments, then there is no way you could have freely chosen to hit your brother. To whatever extent your external and internal environments influenced your choice, they diminished your freedom; you were to that extent—that is, either completely or partially—caused to hit your brother by conditions you did not freely choose and over which you had no control. For instance, if the external and internal environments were sufficient to cause you to want to hit him and your wanting to hit him was sufficient to cause you to choose to hit him and your choosing to hit him was sufficient to cause you to hit him (that is, if, given those external and internal environmental conditions, your choosing to hit him and then subsequently hitting him were inevitable), then you didn't hit him freely. Rather, you were caused to hit him by conditions over which you exercised no free choice and hence over which you had no control, at least none that you could have exercised freely.

Perhaps, though, the external and internal environments in which you found yourself just prior to your hitting your brother merely contributed to your choosing to hit him without absolutely determining that you would choose to hit him. In that case, what else could have contributed to your choosing to hit him? Either there was some additional circumstance that contributed to your choice or there was none. If there was some additional circumstance, then because you didn't freely choose that circumstance either, you couldn't have either chosen freely to hit your brother or subsequently hit him freely. If there was no additional circumstance—that is, if, to some extent, either your wanting to hit your brother or your choice to hit him, or the movement of your arm in hitting him was uncaused— then to that extent your wanting to hit him or your choice to hit him, or the movement of your arm in actually hitting him, was simply a random event.

Random events are not things anyone *does* but merely things that happen. Nothing causes them (that's what it means to say they are random); no one chooses them. They are flukes. It is not up to anyone whether a fluke happens or whether something happens as a consequence of a fluke. Because flukes are not things anyone does, they cannot be things anyone does freely. Therefore, a random event involving you would not be something you do but merely something that happens to you for no reason whatsoever. It would not be up to you whether it happens to you or whether as a consequence of its happening you do something.

So, whether you chose to hit your brother, or whether you just hit him, in neither case did you hit him freely. To whatever extent you were caused to want or choose to hit him, your hitting him was caused by conditions over which you had no control and therefore was not free. To whatever extent you were not caused to want or choose to hit him, your hitting him was a random event over which you had no control and therefore was not free. Thus nothing you do *now* could possibly be done freely because in order for you to do something freely now you must in the past have done something freely for the first time, and there is no way you ever could have done something freely for the first time.

Still, you have a choice. You can *say* that you acted freely provided your action was a consequence of your choice and your choice came about in a normal way, uncoerced by any external agency. Hence, you can *say* that you acted freely even at your fifth birthday party and that your act of reading this now is free. You can stick to that ordinary conception of freedom if you want to. Yet, as before, your sticking to that ordinary conception of freedom would not erase the fact that what you do when (and to whatever extent) your behavior is not simply random is caused by conditions over which no one, and certainly not you, ultimately has any control. If this is freedom, it is less robust than the freedom we ordinarily suppose we have.

Ordinarily we suppose we are free in the sense that *ultimately* what we do is up to us. Freedom of that sort is an illusion. In that ordinary sense of freedom, you have never done anything freely, you can't do anything freely now, and you never will do anything freely.

Want to read on?

KNOWLEDGE

You believe many things. But which, if any, of your beliefs are knowledge?

What *is* knowledge?

Knowledge is not simply belief. If you believe and claim to know something and someone else believes and claims to know the opposite, then at least one of you must be mistaken. When two people believe contradictory things they can't *both* know what they claim to know. That's because one or the other of their beliefs must be false. Merely believing something, no matter how fervently, doesn't make it true. For you to know something, not only must you believe it but it must also be true. But is that all that's required? Is knowledge simply true belief?

Suppose a gambler bets regularly on horses. He always tries to pick winners but he rarely does. Yet he's so full of delusional self-confidence that whenever he places a bet he fervently believes his horse will win. Occasionally, through blind luck, his horse does win. On those rare occasions did the gambler know his horse would win? Of course not. He may have felt completely confident, but that's another matter. To know something you can't just guess it, even if you guess correctly, no matter how confidently you believe your guess. What, then, besides true belief is required for knowledge?

Isn't evidence the answer? That is, to have knowledge don't you have to be connected to the truth of what you believe through the reasons or evidence you have for believing? And don't these reasons or evidence have to be adequate to justify your belief? What makes it so implausible to say that the gambler has knowledge even when he picks a winner is that he doesn't have good reasons or evidence for thinking that the horses he bets on will win. Instead, he wins by luck.

But what is evidence? And when is evidence adequate? These are difficult questions. To keep from getting sidetracked let's just assume for the sake of argument that we know what makes a piece of information evidence for some belief. Let's also assume that we know how much evidence it takes to adequately support that belief. And in assuming we know the latter, let's not set our standards too high. Instead of assuming that to be adequate for knowledge evidence must *conclusively* establish the truth of the belief it supports, let's assume that evidence is adequate when, under the circumstances in which the evidence becomes available, it renders a belief *more likely than not* to be true. If these assumptions are wrong, we can always take them back later. Assuming them for now will simplify the issues and help keep us on track.

Knowledge may be more (or less) than just true belief supported by adequate evidence. But if knowledge is at least that, then one of the things we ought to ask our authorities is what evidence they have for the things they claim to know. And one of the things we ought to ask ourselves, when we accept people as authorities, is what evidence we have that they are competent and trustworthy.

It may seem that when we are dealing with someone who is a well-credentialed authority it would be rather easy to explain what our evidence is that our authority is competent and trustworthy. Remarkably, though, it's rather difficult to explain in a way that makes it obvious that our evidence is adequate. If it seems easy, that's probably because we tend to rest content with providing information that is known, if at all, only indirectly rather than following the thread of evidence all the way to the source. For instance, suppose a seemingly reputable scientist tells you that the east coast of South America and the west coast of Africa used to be connected. You take her word for it. You thereby acquire some beliefs *indirectly;* that is, you acquire them not on the basis of your own experiences of the coastlines of Africa and South America, the Earth's tectonic plates, whatever evidence there is for the theory of continental drift, and so on, but on the basis of her words about her (or someone's) purported experiences of these things. Of course, the scientist's own knowledge might itself be direct or indirect: direct if she sailed along the coasts and made maps, viewed core samples from the ocean floor, and so on, or indirect if she studied someone else's data, charts, and maps. If the latter, and if the scientist really does know what she's talking about, then the information included in those charts, maps, and data must have been known directly by someone. Otherwise, the whole chain of information, leading up to the scientist and ending with you, is a sham.

Hence, if your so-called knowledge is acquired by relying on authority, then it is at best indirect knowledge. But if it really is knowledge, then someone or some group of people must have acquired that knowledge directly. So, with respect to some information that has been conveyed to you by an authority and that you take to be your indirectly acquired knowledge, ask this: Who acquired it directly? Your authority? Or someone else? Under what conditions did they acquire it? How reliably has this information been passed down to you?

Most of the time we don't have a clue about how to answer such questions with respect to the things we accept on authority. We sail through life on an ocean of faith. For instance, returning to our example, why do you believe that the person who told you about continental drift is a scientist? Why do you believe—even if she is a scientist—that on this topic she knows what she's talking about? Perhaps a university catalog lists her name and characterizes her as a scientific authority on continental drift. Why do you believe that the person who told you about the coastlines is the same person named in the catalog? Why do you believe that what is written in the catalog is true? Even if you have good, adequate reasons for believing these things, why do you believe that this scientist, on this occasion, is trustworthy?

Do you believe all of these things because you have direct experience that is adequate to ensure their truth? Or do you believe them on the word of still other authorities? If the latter, then all of the same questions arise with respect to your relationship to these further authorities: Who are they? What is your evidence that they are competent and trustworthy? And so on. This sort of questioning keeps going until you get to people whose supposed knowledge is not based on authority but is direct. In the case of an example like the one we have been considering of the scientific authority on continental drift, who would those people be?

Such questions may seem silly because they raise doubts about whether you know things that it may seem obvious to you that you do know. But we're not asking you to deny that you know what you think you know. We're asking you to think about *how* you know it and by doing that to gain an understanding of what knowledge is. In other words, we're asking you, first, to notice how much of what you think you know is based on someone else's authority, who may in turn be basing what they claim to know on yet someone else's authority, and so on; and, second, we're asking you to persist in questioning *why* you believe that the people you have accepted as your authorities are both competent and trustworthy. We're asking you to do these two things not in order to undermine authority but because it is only by doing them that you can begin to understand what knowledge is. However, if and when you start to take such questions seriously, you will almost surely begin to look at authorities in a more critical and reflective way than you did before. You may even begin to doubt the competency or trustworthiness of some of your authorities and also the wisdom of your tendency to rely unquestioningly on them as much as you do. In other words, you may start thinking more for yourself and relying less on others to do your thinking for you. Such are the all but inevitable consequences of inquiring into the nature of knowledge. That is why authorities rarely encourage you to do it. From their points of view your inquiring into the nature of knowledge is dangerous.

To sum up: Your indirect knowledge, if it really is knowledge, must be based ultimately on someone's direct knowledge. So if the authorities from which you learned what you think you know indirectly really know what they taught you, then someone must have learned it (or the evidence on which it depends for its plausibility) directly. Further, if you know that the authorities that taught you these things are competent and trustworthy, then either you must know this directly or, if you know it on the basis of someone else's authority, then you must know directly that this other authority is competent and trustworthy. In short, when it comes to your knowledge there is a limit to how much you can rely on others. Ultimately, the buck stops with you.

But how does anyone know anything *directly?* Isn't experience the answer? How else could you know something directly but on the basis of your own experience? How else could others know things directly but on the basis of their own experiences? Experience, it seems, must be the answer. But consider the implications.

Most of us think we know a great deal, not just about ourselves but also about the whole universe. We think we know what's real and what's fantasy over an astonishingly large range of topics. Yet if we know everything we think we know ultimately on the basis of our own experience, how could we know so much? Consider, for instance, your so-called knowledge that the universe is huge, expanding, and billions of years old. How could you know this ultimately

on the basis of your own experience? Have you had—are you having—enough experience to justify such beliefs?

You can of course draw upon your past experiences to back up
your present experience, but first you have to know those past experiences really took place. The you-here-and-now reading these words
has no direct access to any experience that you're not presently
having. So how do you know that the experiences you think you remember actually took place? Ultimately you have to know this on the
basis of your *present* experience—in this case, probably your present
memories.

You can't know directly, on the basis of any past experience, that
you've had some particular past experience. Your past experiences
are gone. You may know many things *indirectly* on the basis of your
past experiences. To know things *directly* you have to know them on
the basis of your *present* experience. How else? Even if you pick up a
book of old newspaper clippings, a diary, a photo album, and so on,
these things exist in the present. The things you are right now holding in your hands aren't in the past. Like your hands, they are in the
present. They are here-and-now.

So there could be two kinds of indirect knowledge: knowing
something on the basis of *someone else's* say-so rather than on the
basis of *your own* experience, and knowing something on the basis of
your *past* experience (your present say-so?) rather than on the basis
of your *present* experience.

Knowledge about the past, it would seem, must be based on
what you know directly in the present. You have no direct access to
the past. So if whatever you know is based on what you know directly, and whatever you know directly you must have direct access
to, and the only thing you have direct access to is your present experience, then your present experience is the ultimate source of everything you know.

We don't often look carefully at our experience. In this chapter
we've begun to do just that. Looking at our experience may seem unusual, but it isn't hard to do. You don't have to know any science or
mathematics to do it. You don't have to know anything that you
don't already know. It doesn't even take much effort. Looking carefully at your experience is easy.

Once you've looked, it is also easy to see the enormous gulf between your experience and all the things you believe you know
about yourself and the world. It's quite astonishing to examine your

experience and then compare it even to a radically incomplete list of the things you believe you know. Take a moment to consider your experience right now and compare it to a list of some of the things you believe you know. It's incredible, don't you think, to realize that you may be basing your claim to know so much on the basis of the experiences you're having right now?

Do you see the incredible gulf between your present experience and what you think you know? If you do, then ask yourself this: If what you're experiencing right now is "here," and all those other things you believe you know are "there," how did you get from here to there? What processes of inference did you employ? What reasons do you have for believing those processes of inference are reliable— that they will lead you to the truth, to conclusions that are not just make-believe stories but reality? Do you know the answers to these questions? Does anybody?

One possibility is that science provides the bridge between experience and reality by explaining how experiences are caused. Take, for instance, the experience of watching a sunset. We know directly that we have that experience. What we don't know directly is why we have that experience rather than some other experience or no experience at all. It is widely believed that the function of scientific theories is to provide explanations of experience. Thus your visual experience of the sunset is explained by the sun's emitting rays of light that travel across space and enter your eyes, sending an electrochemical impulse along your optic nerves to your brain. If such scientific theories are the best available explanations of experience, then we might be able to claim legitimately that these theories provide the bridge between experience and reality.

But there are two problems with this answer. One is with the assumption that scientific theories explain experience. It's not that this assumption is false. The example of the sunset illustrates one of the ways in which scientific theories can at least contribute to an explanation of experience. The problem is that science invariably *presupposes* the reality of a world "out there," beyond the reach of our direct experience, that we were trying to use scientific theories to get to. In other words, science gets us to the reality "out there" by presupposing that such a reality exists. Science doesn't get us from "here" to "there"; it gets us from "there" to "here."

Furthermore, science doesn't even really get us to "here." Consider again watching a sunset. Nowhere in the scientific explanation of the visual experience of the sunset does science make the link between physical processes and mental experiences. If you look, for instance, in a textbook on the physiology of our human visual system, you will not find any discussion of subjective mental states. What you will find instead are very complicated physicalistic explanations of the way vision works. These explanations do not link the physiology of vision to mental experiences.

We've been assuming that all knowledge must be based ultimately on direct knowledge and that all direct knowledge must be based on present experience. If this is true, it seems that it's going to be very hard to explain how we know most of the things we think we know, including most of science. So perhaps one or the other of these assumptions is false. That could at least save our belief that we have most of the knowledge we think we have. But at what cost?

If one of our claims about knowledge is false, then either some of our knowledge is only indirect or some of what we know directly we know, not on the basis of our present experience, but in some other way. But what could it mean to have knowledge that is only indirect—that isn't based, ultimately, on direct knowledge? And how could we know something directly that we don't know on the basis of our present experience? What, in that case, could be meant by *directly*?

One possibility is that knowledge rests ultimately on assumptions that are not themselves knowledge. In that case, we could know something even though we don't know it directly. We could know it on the basis of something we merely assume. For instance, perhaps we merely assume that memory is generally reliable (even though we don't *know* this) and thereby know all sorts of things on the basis of memory that we couldn't otherwise know. But if we can get knowledge merely by making assumptions, then it would seem we could know almost anything at all—effortlessly. This conception of knowledge, it seems, would give us by luck what we should acquire only by honest toil. As in the example of the lucky gambler, mere luck would seem to cheapen "knowledge" so much that it would cease being knowledge.

Another possibility is that there is a way of being connected to the truth, and hence of acquiring knowledge, through means other than direct experience. A reliable thermometer, for instance, varies its temperature reading in a way that tracks the correct temperature even though (presumably) it has no direct experience. Perhaps we too, without knowing it, pulse to the hidden rhythms of reality and thereby acquire knowledge without knowing how or why. We know things not because we know that we know them but because, unknown to us, we are reliably connected to the truth.

Although there could perhaps be a kind of knowledge of this sort—knowledge not based on adequate evidence—wouldn't it be a sort of "stupid" or, at best, "lucky" knowledge? If it would be, then, as we have seen, it is questionable whether this sort of "knowledge" would deserve to be called knowledge. And even if, when we had it, it did deserve to be called knowledge, it is hard to see how we could by appeal to it account for all of the knowledge that we think we have. Consider, for instance, what the notion of being "reliably connected to the truth" might mean.

Here's one thing that it could mean: A person's true belief is reliably connected to the truth just in case the person has been caused (at least in part) to have that true belief by the very thing that makes the belief true. Call this account of what it means for a person's true belief to be reliably connected to the truth *the causal account*. To see how the causal account might work in practice and also why one might appeal to it to explain, in the case of some true beliefs that people have, why those beliefs might be thought to be reliably connected to the truth, suppose, for instance, that you believe truly that there is a desk in front of you right now because you see it. In that case, there being a desk in front of you right now is at least a partial cause of your seeing a desk in front of you right now, which is itself at least a partial cause of your believing that there is a desk in front of you right now. Hence, on the causal account, your true belief that there is a desk in front of you right now is reliably connected to the truth.

Fine and dandy for this example. But will this causal account of what it means for a person's true belief to be reliably connected to the truth also work as a general account of knowledge—that is, for all other examples in which it clearly seems that we would have knowledge? There are reasons for thinking that it would not. For instance, suppose that unbeknownst to you an acquaintance of yours—Tom—has an identical twin who lives with him. Suppose further that one day while you're driving to work you happen to see Tom enter the post office. Finally, suppose that your seeing Tom enter the post office causes you to believe that Tom entered the post office. Granted these suppositions, your belief that Tom entered the post office is true. But is your true belief also *reliably connected* to the truth? On the causal account, it would be reliably connected. At least partly because Tom entered the post office, you saw him enter the post office, and at least partly because you saw him enter the post office, you came to believe that he entered the post office. So, on the causal account, your belief that Tom entered the post office would not only be true, but reliably connected to the truth and so, on the causal account, something that you not only believe truly, but also know. But, under the circumstances described, would you really know that Tom entered the post office?

A reason for thinking that under the circumstances described you would not *know* that Tom entered the post office is that under the circumstances described you would have formed the same belief that Tom entered the post office had it not been Tom but his identical twin who you had seen enter the post office. It would seem then that while you formed a true belief on this occasion, you did so in a way and in circumstances in which your belief might easily have been false. In other words, you formed a true belief, but it was just lucky that your belief turned out to be true. Presumably, beliefs that turn out to be true as a consequence of luck are not reliably connected to the truth, at least not in the right sort of way for them to count as knowledge. Hence, this example suggests that satisfaction of the causal account would not guarantee that true beliefs are reliably connected to the truth in the right sort of way for them to count as knowledge.

A different sort of example can be used, even more dramatically, to illustrate how satisfaction of the causal condition would reward luck in allowing some beliefs to count as knowledge. Suppose, for instance, that a gambler who doesn't have any inside information places the following sort of $2 bet on two consecutive horse races: He will win $20 if he picks the winner in either race or in both races, but otherwise he will lose. In placing his bet the gambler picks Gumshoe to win the first race and Tagalong to win the second. He picks these horses not on the basis of good evidence that they will win but for the most frivolous of reasons: His mother is named Gumshoe and his sister is named Tagalong. Suppose further that before the first race begins the gambler is called away from the track and does not return until after the end of the second race. While he is away he forgets what sort of bet he placed on the first two races and then forms the mistaken belief that he placed a regular $2 bet just on the first race and that what he bet was that Gumshoe would win it. As it happens, while he is away and unknown to him, Gumshoe does win the first race and Tagalong finishes last in the second. On returning to the track and still not knowing the results of either race, the gambler goes to the cashier's window and presents his ticket. Without speaking a word the cashier gives him $20, from which the gambler infers that Gumshoe won the first race.

In this example, the gambler, it would seem, is on the causal account reliably connected to the truth of what he believes. He believes Gumshoe won the first race, and because Tagalong lost in the second the cashier would not have paid him $20 for his ticket unless Gumshoe had won in the first. But should we say that the gambler *knew* that Gumshoe won in the first race? He believed that Gumshoe won, it was true that Gumshoe won, and the way in which he came to that belief was on the causal account reliably connected to what made the belief true. Yet most of us would be reluctant to say that the gambler knew Gumshoe won in the first race. Although the gambler may on the causal account have been reliably connected to what made his belief that Gumshoe won true, he was just lucky to be reliably connected. The two examples just given suggest that true beliefs can satisfy the causal account, yet not be reliably connected to the truth in the right way for them to count as instances of knowledge.

Different examples suggest that true beliefs can be instances of knowledge even though they don't satisfy the requirements of the causal account. One of the things you know, for instance, is that there is no hippopotamus that is smaller than an ant. So, assuming that the causal condition were true and a requirement of knowledge, what would be the causal connection between the *fact* that there is no hippopotamus that is smaller than an ant and your *belief* that there is no hippopotamus that is smaller than an ant? It's hard to say. Or, consider mathematical knowledge, say, your knowledge that $7 + 5 = 12$ or so-called subjunctive knowledge, such as knowledge you might have, say, that were it to rain they would call off the game. How would such true beliefs, which you also know (or might know) to be true, satisfy the requirements of the causal account? The answer, it would seem, is that they wouldn't satisfy it. But if such beliefs really are (or could be) knowledge and they wouldn't satisfy the causal account, then it can't be right that a person's true belief is reliably connected to the truth, and hence knowledge, just in case (that is, if and only if) the person has been caused (at least in part) to have that true belief by the very thing that makes the belief true.

Perhaps there is a way of explaining what's meant by being reliably connected to the truth that avoids such difficulties. Otherwise it's tempting to suppose that we cannot account for knowledge if we omit the requirement that one have adequate evidence for what one believes and simply substitute for it the requirement that one's belief be reliably connected to the truth. For instance, in the case of the example of the gambler, the problem, it seems, is that the gambler did not have adequate reasons or evidence for his belief that Gumshoe won in the first race. If that's what keeps his belief that Gumshoe won from counting as knowledge, then being reliably connected to what makes your belief true may not be enough for knowledge. And that would lead us straight back to the problems that we sought to escape by going from an evidential to a reliability account of knowledge.

The key to addressing the puzzles we have been considering is to discover what things we know *directly* and how we know them. Yet it's not easy to explain how we could know anything directly except perhaps what we are experiencing in the present moment. But that does not leave us with very much. Knowledge, which must ultimately be based on direct experience, requires that we go beyond experience. In other words, knowledge requires *theory*. Without theory, we, who ultimately are nowhere and no one, know almost nothing at all.

But how do we know whether our theories are true?

6

A fundamental tenet of many theological systems, both Western and Eastern, is that we can connect directly (and absolutely) to the most real thing: God. According to them, God is the reality underlying the reality of everything, including both experience and the external world. So if science can't build a bridge from experience to reality, perhaps religion can.

Might the knowledge that God exists provide the necessary bridge between experience and reality—between our subjective mental states and the external world? Perhaps. But only if we know that God exists. Many people believe they know that God exists. But they may be mistaken—even if God does exist. As we saw in the last chapter, your true belief might be based not on adequate evidence but on irrelevant considerations. For a belief to be knowledge, the belief must not only be true, it must also satisfy some further condition. A plausible candidate for such a condition is that the belief must be based on adequate evidence.

So we need to ask, is there *adequate evidence* that God exists? There certainly seems to be: the universe. The mere fact that the universe exists suggests that the universe must have come from somewhere. Everything must come from somewhere. Tables, chairs, trees, and so on, do not just pop into existence out of nowhere. Tables and chairs are made by people, trees come from seeds, and so on. The universe, too, must have come from somewhere—it must have had an external cause. Everything must have had an external cause. And the only thing that could have caused the universe is God.

But this apparently obvious answer creates an equally obvious problem: If everything must come from somewhere, where does God come from? Perhaps we don't need to explain where God comes from because God, unlike the universe, exists without any external cause. In that case, however, we've blatantly contradicted the very assumption that made us suppose that the universe must have been caused by God—namely, the assumption that everything must come from somewhere. Without that assumption, the existence of the universe is no longer evidence for God.

Perhaps, though, God—unlike everything else, including the universe—does not need an external cause. However, if we're going to assume that God is an exception to this rule, why not just assume more simply that the universe is an exception to this rule? A fundamental tenet of evidence and reasoning is that, all else being equal, a simpler hypothesis should be preferred to a more complex one. The hypothesis that the universe can exist without an external cause requires just one entity—the universe—plus the assumption that the universe is self-caused. The God hypothesis requires *two* entities—the universe and God—plus the assumption that God is self-caused. Thus the hypothesis that the universe can exist without an external cause is simpler than the God hypothesis. Even if it weren't simpler, however, unless we have good reason for adopting one standard for the universe (that is, the universe must have an external cause) and then a different standard for God (that is, God does not have to have an external cause), any conclusion based on such a double standard is not knowledge.

Do we have any reason to adopt one standard for the universe and a different standard for God? Perhaps the universe, because it consists of material objects, requires an external cause. Material objects obviously come into and go out of existence—they are impermanent—and hence are the sorts of things that require an external cause. God, on the other hand, is popularly supposed to be a spiritual being and therefore permanent. So it may seem that God does not require an external cause.

Although it may be true that the universe is impermanent, how do we know that it requires an external cause? Indeed, as we shall see in the chapter on the cosmos, some scientific evidence indicates that the universe does not require an external cause. Unless someone can establish the limitations of the universe as a whole, it would be presumptuous to point to the cosmos and declare it incapable of existing without an external cause.

Furthermore, how do we know that God, just by virtue of being a spiritual entity, must be permanent? To know that, we would have to have enough evidence about spiritual entities to know their nature.

But as we shall discover (in this chapter as well as the one on death), we don't have such evidence. So if it is presumptuous to claim to know the limitations of the cosmos, it is even more presumptuous to claim to know enough about the nature of spiritual beings to know that God is permanent.

Is there any other possible evidence that God exists? Again, the universe—this time not the mere fact that it exists, but that it is so well ordered. The precise operation of the solar system, the complex biology of human life, the breathtaking molecular structure of plants—how could all this be the result of mere chance? That it is mere accident, the result not of design but of the unconscious evolution of matter, would be a fluke too incredible to be believed. We ought, therefore, to believe instead in the existence of an intelligent designer: God.

But if all order, without exception, requires a designer, then God, too, requires a designer. If God were the intelligent designer of the universe, God would have to be even more perfectly ordered than the universe. But if God were even more perfectly ordered than the universe, and God could exist without an external designer, then why not the universe? Claiming that God's order does not require an external designer, whereas the universe's order *does* require it, once more employs an unjustified double standard.

Again, it is tempting to believe that God is special—that God, unlike the universe, does not require an external designer. Maybe God is special in this way. But how can anyone *know* that the universe requires an external designer? And again, as we shall see in the chapter on the cosmos, some current theories in physics claim the universe designed itself. What entitles anyone to claim to know in advance of examining these theories that they must be wrong? Finally, which is simpler: the idea of a well-ordered universe somehow ordering itself, or the idea of a well-ordered universe plus an even better-ordered (and self-ordered) being who ordered it?

Even if we accept that the universe must be the product of an intelligent designer, what evidence do we have that the designer has the attributes we ordinarily attribute to God? How do we know, for instance, whether the designer is good or bad? We can't usually determine the moral qualities of artists by looking at their paintings. How do we know if the universe had one designer or many? We can't tell by looking at the pyramids how many architects contributed to their design. Indeed, how can we know if the supposed designer or designers of the universe still exist? Watches often outlast their makers.

All the reasons we've considered thus far for the existence of God clearly do not establish that God exists. It is surprising, then, and somewhat disturbing, that these reasons are so often presented as if they were good reasons. And there is something even more disturbing about them. The reasons we've considered begin by confronting the mystery in front of our noses—the mystery of the existence and order of the universe around us—and then quickly move in a direction that takes us away both from our experience and from the mystery itself.

The universe is a marvelous and puzzling place that can be observed from your own backyard. The hypotheses we've considered about God do not solve the puzzles but complicate them. Worse, they take you away from the familiar realm of your experience and transport you into the abstract and arcane realm of theological theory. The walls and ceilings of great cathedrals may be beautiful, but you can't see through the windows, and the high vaults obscure the sky. The awesome mystery of the universe cannot be contained in a building—yet any child staring at the open sky can be awestruck.

Is there any other possible evidence that God exists? Numerous holy books not only claim that God exists but also describe God's nature. How could there be so many holy books, in so many different cultures, separated by such great gulfs of time and space if God did not exist?

If these numerous holy books prove anything about God, however, they prove too much. For not only do they disagree with each other about God's nature, they even disagree about whether God exists. You will find this to be true even if you consider only the holy books associated with the major religions. Theravada Buddhist holy books, for instance, go so far as to claim implicitly that God does *not* exist. In any event, even if the holy books agreed with each other, what would that show? By itself, nothing. You can't generate evidence that God exists by taking a vote. At one time almost everybody believed the Earth is flat.

There is, however, one respect in which all the world's holy books are alike: They are all filled with miracle stories that are supposed to provide evidence for the particular religion that the stories help to sustain. However, because the world's religions differ drastically in their beliefs about God, if the miracle stories of one religion count as evidence for the claims of that religion, then they also count as evidence against the claims of the other religions.

Even if we accept the miracle stories, how do we know to what, or to whom, we should attribute the miracles? If God is responsible, which God? The Hindu God? The Christian God? The Muslim God? For all we know, isn't it possible that the people who supposedly witnessed the miracles caused the miracles themselves through some hidden power unknown even to them? Consider, for instance, so-called miracle cures: Why deny the possibility that we have the power to cure ourselves?

Most people who accept miracle stories in holy books accept only those in *some* holy books. Hindus, for instance, rarely find the miracle stories in Christian holy books, such as the story that Jesus changed water into wine merely by willing the change, persuasive. Christians rarely find miracle stories in Hindu holy books, such as the story that Krishna transformed into a thousand replicas of himself so as better "to sport" with the milkmaids, persuasive. Why? Most people who are religious believe in the religion of their parents. But beliefs that depend on accidents of birth prove nothing. Just imagine, for instance, that the Pope's parents had been Hindu rather than Catholic and that he had been raised in India rather than in the West. In that case his religious beliefs would probably be different and he wouldn't have become Pope. He probably would accept miracle stories he now rejects and reject miracle stories he now accepts.

Religious people are often blind to the extent to which social conditioning influences where they draw the line between what seems acceptable and what seems just plain superstitious. For instance, following the long-standing Christian tradition of trying to wean people away from superstitious pagan beliefs, the current Pope, a few years ago, lectured Africans on the superstitious character of some of their native religious practices. He then celebrated Holy Mass. Suddenly, according to his Catholic beliefs, the ordinary bread in his hands, through the ritual of his uttering a few words, *literally* became the body of Christ, which he then ate, and the ordinary wine in his chalice *literally* became the blood of Christ, which he then drank! The Africans were dumbfounded.

If holy books don't provide adequate evidence that God exists, what about the personal religious experiences that, down through the ages and in many diverse cultures, have been reported by mystics? Many mystics claim to have experienced God. Do their experiences provide adequate evidence that God exists? It depends on whether the best explanation of the mystic's experience requires us to suppose that God exists. If it doesn't, then the mystic's belief that he or she has experienced God is not knowledge.

Consider an analogy. Many people down through the ages and in many diverse cultures have had the experience of apparently communicating with dead relatives. Does the fact that people have had these experiences prove that ghosts exist? It all depends on whether the best explanation of these experiences requires us to suppose that ghosts exist. The problem is that there are other ways to explain such experiences: fraud, hallucination, and so on. For instance, the people might have hallucinated their "communications" due to chemical changes in their brains brought on by the shock and grief of losing a loved one. As long as such natural explanations are at least as likely as ghost explanations, such experiences do not provide adequate evidence that ghosts exist.

So too with the mystic. One way to explain the mystic's apparent experience of God is to suppose that the mystic actually did experience God. Another way is to suppose that the mystic hallucinated experiencing God due to chemical changes brought about by fasting, meditation, or some other unknown but natural cause. So the question is whether we have more reason to believe the mystic's explanation than we have to believe an alternative, naturalistic explanation.

We know very little about how the brain works in bringing about our experiences. For example, no one knows precisely why dreams occur or why we have exactly the dreams we do. Yet ordinarily we don't suppose that any of the characters in our dreams are supernatural entities. We suppose that somehow or other dreams can be explained naturalistically; we just don't know how yet.

If we don't even know how to explain ordinary dreams, it's not surprising that we don't know how to explain exotic mystical experiences. The fact that we don't know how to explain either sort of experience doesn't mean we won't someday be able to explain them naturalistically. For the mystic's experience to provide adequate evidence for the existence of God, the mystic, or someone, would have to show that the religious explanation of the experience is more likely to be true than that there is some yet unknown naturalistic explanation. No one has ever been able to show this.

Next, we must turn to something we have not yet considered: the possibility of evidence *against* the existence of God. If God exists, why is there so much seemingly unnecessary suffering? God is supposed to be all-knowing, all-powerful, and perfectly good. So either God doesn't know about the suffering (in which case "God" is not all-knowing and therefore is not God) or else God knows about the suffering but can't stop it (in which case "God" is not all-powerful and therefore is not God). Or perhaps God knows about the suffering and *can* stop it but chooses not to (in which case "God" is not perfectly good and therefore is not God).

A possible reply involves an appeal to the concept of free will. God doesn't cause suffering; people do. God chose to create people with free will. What people do with their own free will is their responsibility, not God's. Given a choice between a world in which there is free will and suffering, and a world in which there is no free will and no suffering, the former is the better choice. God made the better choice.

This reply has several problems. First, suffering is often caused not by people but by nature—by so-called acts of God: floods, earthquakes, tornados, hurricanes, tidal waves, (many) famines, plagues, birth defects, diseases, and so on. Why couldn't we have all the free will we now have without so many natural disasters and thus without the suffering they cause? It seems strange to suppose that if there were fewer earthquakes, there would thereby be less free will.

Second, even with our merely human intelligence, it is easy to imagine how we could have as much free will as we now have without as much suffering as we now endure. For example, God—because God is supposed to be omnipotent—could have created a world in which people are less easily injured. Then, even if people behaved as unwisely as many now do, the consequences would not involve nearly as much suffering. Or God could intervene occasionally to make things go better without interfering with free will. For instance, suppose that God had altered the ocean winds just enough to blow the Conquistadors off course, a small feat in comparison to the creation of the cosmos. What reason is there to think that this act of God, and the subsequent survival of all those natives of Latin America who were slaughtered mercilessly or died of European diseases, would have resulted in a net loss of free will in the world?

Third, it's not enough to *have* free will. Our free will would have to be of a kind that absolves God of responsibility for our actions. In

HÆLLO

other words, our free acts would have to not be caused by circumstances around us, for instance, by genetic and environmental factors ultimately caused by God. Because if God is behind our actions—if God created a long chain of events that God foresaw would ensure that we do whatever we do—then how could our actions be free in a way that absolves God of responsibility? In that case God at least would have to share responsibility for our actions. After all, God would have made us perform them.

Furthermore, what evidence do we have that our actions are uncaused? The evidence from psychology and biology suggests that all our actions are caused, ultimately, not by us but by genetic and environmental circumstances. How could anyone claim to know, in light of this evidence, that people have the sort of free will required to absolve God (who, according to religious doctrine, created the genetic and environmental circumstances) of responsibility for our actions?

Finally, an omnipotent God could have created a world in which people freely chose to do good rather than evil *as often* as they do in this world. Indeed, God, if God exists, did choose to create such a world: this one. Thus God, it would seem, could also have chosen to create a world in which people freely chose to do good rather than evil *more often* than they do in this world. Such a better world would not be a world without suffering. But it would be a world with *less* suffering. Isn't it possible that it would also be a world with just as much free will as this world? To know that God exists, we would have to have evidence that excludes this possibility. If we can't show that this possibility has been excluded, then "God," it seems, is responsible for not having chosen a better world and therefore is responsible for the unnecessary suffering in this world—and hence is not God.

We began by asking whether there is adequate evidence that God exists. If there is any such evidence, we haven't yet found it. Perhaps, then, the best response is to appeal to faith. To have faith in God is to believe in God in the absence of adequate evidence. Many religious experts today concede that there is no adequate evidence for the existence of God and hence that one must believe on faith or not at all. But notice that if the question is whether we can *know* that God exists, anyone who claims that we *must* believe on faith is in effect conceding that the answer is "No." Of course, the Hindu might *claim to know* that the Hindu gods exist, just as the Muslim might claim to know that the Muslim God exists, and the Christian might claim to know that the Christian God exists. But on this point—if religious belief is based on faith—the Hindu, the Muslim, and the Christian are all simply mistaken. Faith is not knowledge. Furthermore, faith cuts both ways. One might just as well believe on faith that God does *not* exist.

The believer might appeal to therapeutic considerations, such as that belief in God is psychologically healthier. But many atheists appeal to the same sort of considerations to argue that belief in God is psychologically unhealthy. Some atheists even claim that belief in God is dangerous because faith provides no reason for preferring the God of one religion over the God of another. The Hindu, for instance, is just as entitled to believe on faith in Krishna as the Christian is entitled to believe on faith in Jesus, as the Muslim is entitled to believe on faith in Allah, and so on. When people can't settle their fundamental differences rationally, they almost invariably resort to violence. Historically, and even today, religious differences are a potent source of social violence. When people—whether theists or atheists—attach themselves more closely to answers than to life, their answers become not solutions but problems.

The believer's response to the mystery of existence is to invoke a mysterious word—*God*. Such a move does little to help us understand ourselves and the universe better. Mysterious words, like mysterious answers, don't solve mysteries. They merely obscure them by putting a verbal barrier between us and the unknown. Such verbal barriers—religious or otherwise—can diminish our feelings of puzzlement and insecurity at finding ourselves without answers. But there is a big difference between confronting an enigma directly and covering it up. The believer's mystery is a mystery once removed.

It is not just believers who regularly try to cover up mystery. Atheists too regularly try to cover it up. And both groups, when they try to hide mystery, try to hide it in basically the same way—by pretending to know more than they actually know. Believers pretend to know that God exists, that God created the world, and so on. Atheists pretend to know that there are no truths beyond scientific truths—that is, beyond those of the natural and social sciences, mathematics, technical know-how, historical studies, facts of everyday life, and so on.

Suppose believers and atheists got together and decided to stop pretending to know more than they actually know. What, then, would they claim to know? Because they would no longer be pretending, such a believer and such an atheist would be the most intelligent sort of believer and atheist. So, what we are asking is, What would the most intelligent sort of believer and the most intelligent sort of atheist claim to know? Perhaps just this: that there are scientific truths and there is the mystery.

REALITY

Theological concepts, like "God," and scientific concepts, like "space-time continuum," are embedded in elaborate theories developed to explain the reality we experience—the reality we see and feel directly. Reasons for believing in such theories, it would seem, must be based ultimately on experience. So rather than using theories as our point of departure (we'll consider them again at the end of the next chapter), let's stick to our experience and see if there is a way of getting from it to an understanding of reality.

Do we directly experience the real world? Most of us believe we do. We may not know who we are or what makes *us* real but we are here, right now, in the universe, experiencing the reality of things like tables and chairs. What makes *them* real?

Take, for instance, an ordinary chair. A chair is one of the most obvious, most concrete, least theoretical, and least controversial examples of a real object. We all know what a chair is. A chair is so familiar to us, so obviously real, that its very obviousness masks the mystery of the chair's reality. If we were talking instead about quarks or black holes, we wouldn't forget the mystery. But because everyone knows what chairs are and that they are real, we assume we all know what it is that *makes* a chair real.

You may be sitting on a chair right now; probably you can see one. Consider the chair. What makes it a real chair? The question isn't what makes it a real *chair*. The question is what makes it a *real* chair—what its *being real* consists in. In other words, the question isn't what makes your chair a real chair as opposed, for instance, to a real table, but, rather, what makes your chair a real chair as opposed to an unreal—a hallucinatory or imagined—chair. If we can understand the reality of a simple object like a chair—what it is that makes it real—then we may be on the way to understanding reality.

This much, at least, seems clear: An unreal chair—a hallucinatory or imagined chair—exists only in our minds. Real chairs exist in the world independently of our minds. So removing the contribution our minds make to our experience of the chair might help us to understand what makes a chair real. What is that contribution?

To find out, let's look more carefully at our experience. When we experience a chair, we see it, feel it, and think about it. But what is "seeing"? What is "feeling"? What is "thinking"?

The thinking component of your experience is clearly not "out there." Your thoughts may be about something that exists out there independently of your mind, but your thoughts themselves exist only in your mind. Your thought that the chair is comfortable or pretty, for instance, obviously exists only in your mind. Many, perhaps all, of the qualities you attribute to the chair also exist only in your mind. The qualities of comfort and beauty exist only in your mind (or at least apart from the chair). Someone else may find the chair uncomfortable and ugly. The chair by itself is neither comfortable nor uncomfortable, neither pretty nor ugly.

Suppose, however, you're thinking that the chair is made of atoms. Obviously that thought is in your mind. But the atoms of the chair are not in your mind. Notice, however, that unless you're looking at the chair through an electron microscope, you don't directly experience the individual atoms of the chair. That the chair is made of atoms—even that the dots you see through an electron microscope *are atoms*—is a theory. Ordinarily you don't directly experience the chair as atoms. You directly experience the chair as a chair.

You may be thinking, on the other hand, not that the chair is pretty or that it's made of atoms but, rather, "the chair has the qualities I see and feel directly—the chair is brown, smooth, solid, and so on—and these qualities exist both in my experience *and* in the chair." Is this true?

Before we can find out, we must first clarify what we're searching for. What might a mental contribution to seeing and feeling be like? The idea of such a contribution is unfamiliar. So before we consider qualities such as brownness, smoothness, and solidity, let's first consider a clear, uncontroversial example of how we sometimes, perhaps without realizing it, make a mental contribution to our experience.

As you sit on the chair, you're also seeing and feeling this book. You're looking at this page. Now look at the following word:

Chair

Just look at it. Don't think about it. It may help to look at each letter in the word, left to right and then right to left. Stare at the word
for a minute or two without moving your eyes. Blink if your eyes
start to water, but otherwise keep your eyes as still as possible and,
without thinking, focus right on the word.

What happens? If you look long enough, the word *chair* and its
meaning both dissolve into other words and other meanings, like *ha,
hair,* and *air,* which then in turn dissolve into the letters *c, h, a, i,* and *r.*

Where then did the word *chair* and its meaning go? Where did
the other words and their meanings go? Nowhere. The words and
their meanings were never there on the page, existing independently
of your mind. You created that illusion by grouping the letters and
then assigning a meaning to them. The letters by themselves are not
a word. Rather, the word and its meaning are created when you
group the letters to create meaning. Meaning is not discovered by
you and it does not exist out there on the page independently of your
mind. Meaning is made by you and depends for its existence on your
mind.

What happens if you keep on looking? First, the letters dissolve
into shapes. The *c,* for instance, instead of being a letter, might become a cartoon nose or ear; the *h* might become a chair, and so on.
Then, these interpreted shapes further dissolve into uninterpreted
shapes—into blots on the page. The letters—which are interpretations of inkblots—were never "out there" any more than were the
"noses" or "ears." The most that was out there independently of
your mind were *uninterpreted* shapes: blots. You're looking at
inkblots right now but seeing letters and words and sentences and
thus creating meaning. But there are only uninterpreted blots on the
page. What binds the blots together and interprets them? You do.

Now consider what happens when you repeat the word *chair*
silently in your mind. Just say *chair* to yourself over and over. Don't
look at anything—close your eyes. In other words, do with the
sound of the word *chair* in your mind exactly what you just did with
the printed word *chair.* Right now, before you go on to the next paragraph, spend a minute repeating the word silently to yourself.

What happens? The longer you listen to yourself repeating the
word *chair,* the more the meaning begins to dissolve. First the one
meaning turns ambiguous—you hear the other words that compose
the word *chair,* like *hair* and *air.* Next, the unity of that mental sound
dissolves as the end of one repetition slurs into the next. Eventually,

all meaning dissolves. You hear just uninterpreted mental imagery—sounds without meaning.

The technique of just looking at the written word *chair* and just listening to the auditory image *chair* separates our experience of the word *chair* into its components in a way that reveals the contribution we make to our experience. It makes clear exactly how our minds can covertly color our experience.

The word *chair*, of course, isn't a real chair. Words are concepts, and concepts depend on our minds for their existence. We want to know about real chairs—about reality. Is the chair you actually experience really "out there" or—as seems obviously false—does it, too, depend for its existence on your mind?

Let's examine your experience and find out. Are the qualities you experience directly properties of your chair? We've seen that the symbols referring to that chair depend for their existence *as symbols* on your mind. To what extent, if at all, do brownness, smoothness, solidity, and so on depend on your mind? Suppose we try to do to your experience of the chair what we just did to the word *chair* and try to remove whatever mental contribution you may covertly be making to your experience of the chair. Just look for several minutes at your chair. What happens?

Your visual experience changes. Just as your visual experience of the written word *chair* dissolved into its component parts, so also your visual experience of the chair dissolves into its component parts. First, your visual experience dissolves into the experience of legs, seat, back, and so on. Then, if you keep looking without thinking and without letting your eyes move, these components of your experience dissolve into further components—ultimately, into colors and shapes. Colors and shapes are all that is left of your visual experience of the chair once your mental contribution has been stripped away. Ironically, it's your eyes and your thoughts *moving* that makes your visual experience of the chair seem so stable.

Ordinarily, when we look at a chair, our experience has a unity and stability. Our experience doesn't dissolve into its uninterpreted components; we don't see just colors and shapes. We see, for instance, a brown leather chair. Why? Because we're not *just* looking. We're looking and thinking. Looking *and* thinking is different from *just* looking.

What we just did to the seeing component of your experience can also be done to the feeling component. First, though, we must

rate the seeing and feeling components from each other. Ordi-
y, when you look at and feel the corner of your chair, we say
yｏｕ are both looking at and feeling the same thing: the corner of the
chair. But this way of speaking obscures the fact that the visual component of your experience—your seeing—is radically different from
the tactile component of your experience—your feeling.

What do you *see* directly when you look at the corner of your
chair? Ultimately, you see only uninterpreted color patches. What do
you *feel* directly when you touch the corner of your chair? Ultimately, only "raw feels"—that is, the uninterpreted experiences of
touch, like hot, wet, smooth, soft, and so on. These raw feels are colorless and therefore are not color patches. Similarly, color patches
are not hot, wet, smooth, soft, and so on in the way raw feels are. We
sometimes use the same language for both visual and tactile experiences. For instance, we say that a color is soft or hot. But the visual
experience we call *soft* or *hot* is radically different from the tactile experience we call by the same names.

So color patches are very different from raw feels. And both
color patches and raw feels are different from the thing they are experiences of—in this case, the corner of the chair. We obscure these
fundamental differences by using the same words to describe all
three: color patch, raw feel, and chair. When we are both feeling and
seeing the corner of the chair, we say that we are directly experiencing the chair. This is how we forge in our minds the image of reality
that we then project onto our experience.

Consider now what happens to your tactile experience of the
chair if you just feel without thinking—that is, without interpretation. The experience you would ordinarily describe as the experience
of feeling your chair ultimately dissolves into a conglomerate of uninterpreted raw feels.

We rarely *just* look or *just* feel. Ordinarily, thinking—interpreting—is added to the visual and tactile components of experience.
What we ordinarily regard as direct experience is thus a mixture, on
the one hand, of seeing, feeling, hearing, and so on and, on the other,
of thought. We're so used to both sensing reality and at the same
time interpreting it that we don't notice the thinking part—we don't
notice the mental contribution we make to our experience.

Experiencing chairs the way we ordinarily experience them,
which includes thinking, tends to solidify experience into a concrete
image we call *reality*. Looking *and* thinking (what we call *looking*) or

feeling *and* thinking (what we call *feeling*) solidifies your experience of the chair. Just looking or just feeling dissolves your experience of the chair into its component parts.

What about just *thinking*? Just thinking about our perception of the chair supports the view that most of the qualities we directly experience when we experience the chair are not properties of the chair by itself but depend for their existence on our experience. Think, for instance, about what is going on when you are seeing and feeling the chair. Suppose you see brown and feel solidity. What do you see and what do you feel?

Color is produced by the reflection of light from the surface of the chair. You see brown, or whatever color your particular chair may be, because the material of the chair absorbs light from some wavelengths and reflects others. The wavelengths that get reflected produce pressure—patterns of stimulation—on the back of your retinas. The light stops there. Your eyes are not windows. Your eyes are like radio antennae that pick up wavelengths, convert them into an electrical signal, and then send it along to the receiver. Your brain is the receiver.

The pressure produced by the light on the back of your retina causes electrical impulses to fire along your optic nerve. Your brain receives these impulses and interprets them as brown. The light that produced the pressure is itself uncolored. Light is merely a wave. Just as there are longer and shorter waves on the ocean, so there are longer and shorter wavelengths of light. The difference between red light and blue light is in the length of the waves. Color is not a property of waves; it depends on the thing interpreting the waves. Your eyes receive the wavelengths, and your optic nerve transmits electrochemical signals to your brain, which then interprets those signals as color.

Thus, on one level, grass can be said to be more "red" than green because grass absorbs the "red" wavelengths. What you see is what the grass repels: green. On a deeper level, the grass can be said to be colorless. Wavelengths are just that—wavelengths. *We* interpret the lengths of the colorless waves as red, green, yellow, or mauve. Strictly speaking, it's our brains that make such interpretations. Color is not out there—it depends for its existence on us.

What about solidity? You feel the solidity of the chair. But is the chair solid? Perhaps—but consider what the chair's solidity amounts to. The chair is composed of atoms. Between and within atoms there is mostly empty space. If the nucleus of an atom were the size of a marble and placed at the center of the largest football stadium, the electrons would be specks of dust whirling in the uppermost bleachers. Between atoms there is also lots of empty space—even more than between the electrons of an atom and its nucleus. As a famous physicist recently put it during a jam-packed lecture, "The universe is incredibly empty." No one laughed.

We say things like, "You touched a solid chair." But the chair's solidity is questionable, and the closest you get to actually touching the chair is the point at which the force of repulsion between the atoms in your fingers and the atoms of the chair stops your movement. You never directly touch the atoms of the chair. All we ever touch directly is the force of repulsion. Trying to touch, we only repel. We are never physically in direct contact with each other or, for that matter, with any object in the universe.

How do the forces you experience when you think you're feeling the chair produce what you call *solid, smooth, warm,* and so on? Just as in the case of color, these forces initiate a complex series of interactions that begins in the tips of your fingers and ends in your brain's interpreting those forces to create what we call *experience.*

Solidity, color, warmth, smoothness, and so on, are not "out there" independently of your mind. The most that's really "out there" are colorless dots in empty space. Just as you are right now connecting the inkblots on this page, grouping them together to create words and meanings, so you connect the dots you see when you look at the chair, grouping them together in your mind to create colors and solidity. We paint by numbers. But who are we? Are *we* real? What if we, too, are just colorless dots in empty space—space that is itself ultimately nowhere?

What, then, is reality? We began with one of the most uncontroversial examples of a real object—a chair—and tried to understand through examining our experience what it is about the chair that makes it real. On examination, however, we found that none of the components into which our experience of the chair dissolved—seeing, touching, and so on—exist "out there" independently of the mind. Is the answer, then, that the so-called real objects that we directly experience—chairs, tables, and so on—are not "out there" but depend on our minds for their existence?

This may seem too bizarre to be true. Clearly, thought is in the mind. Experience, on the other hand, as we saw, may include a thought component—interpretation—and depend for its existence on our minds. But experience, we ordinarily believe, is caused by something "out there" in the real world that exists independently of our minds and affects our sense organs. Experience, we ordinarily believe, differs from thought in that it provides a kind of bridge between our minds and reality. Perhaps if we understood experience better we might be able to cross that bridge and discover the true nature of reality.

EXPERIENCE

8

Suppose you burn yourself on the stove. What happens? First there is pain. Then perhaps anger. Then finally the realization that you were careless. The pain is a sensation, the anger is an emotion, and the realization that you were careless is a thought. All three—sensation, emotion, and thought—are components of your experience.

The pain in your finger is clearly a sensation. The thought that you've been careless, on the other hand, seems not to be a sensation. Thinking about burning yourself on the stove, though it might produce discomfort, is different from the actual feeling of burning yourself on a real stove.

What about the emotion of anger? Emotion seems to be a mixture of sensation and thought. Anger at burning yourself is partly a sensation in your body, a feeling of agitation and perhaps of warmth. But it is also partly a thought, in this case (perhaps) the thought that you shouldn't have been so careless.

What, then, is it about experience that makes us think we are in touch with reality? Isn't it the sensation component, which in turn is composed of seeing, hearing, touching, tasting, and smelling? Of the three components of our experience—sensation, emotion, and thought—sensation seems to put us directly in touch with the world "out there," with reality, because ordinarily our sensations are directly caused by the actions of real, physical objects on our sense organs.

Sensation may also be colored by our minds—but less, it seems, than either emotion or thought. When you have a sensation, thoughts may be associated with it. But these thoughts are not the sensation itself. You *sense* sensations. You *think* thoughts. You might subsequently think about your pain or your hunger or your pleasure. You're doing that right now—you're thinking about sensations—but you're probably not feeling pain or hunger or pleasure by thinking about these sensations. If you do feel pain, it's because you're actually feeling it, not because you're thinking about it. Pains hurt. Thoughts don't. Or do they?

Can thoughts hurt? Sometimes they can. Suppose you're thinking of the death of a loved one. This thought can cause intense pain. Although a thought isn't itself pain, it can *cause* pain. That's the crucial distinction. Pains are themselves pains. Thoughts aren't themselves pains. If thoughts are painful, it's because they cause pain. But *being* pain and *causing* pain are different.

So does sensation really put us in touch with the world out there—with reality? To see whether it does, we shall have to separate, if we can, those aspects of sensation caused by the outside world from those caused by our own minds. To do that, we must clarify exactly what our sensations consist of. What then does the sensation of pain consist of? This is not a question about what causes pain, nor is it a question about what pain causes. Rather, it is a question about what pain is in and of itself, separate from the things that cause pain and the things pain causes. For example, thought sometimes causes pain, but thought is still distinct from the pain it causes. Similarly, pain sometimes causes thought, but pain is distinct from the thought it causes.

Let's assume, then, that pain is something separate from the things that cause it and the things it causes. What then is pain? We suggested above that pain is one thing and thought another. But is the distinction between pain and thought as neat as that? Perhaps not. Perhaps sensations always include a thought component. And perhaps thoughts always include a sensation component.

It is easy to see that many thoughts have a sensation component. Consider what goes on in your consciousness when you daydream. Daydreaming is a form of thought. We often think through a problem by daydreaming about it. When we daydream, we make up visual fantasies and watch them unfold. So daydreaming has a sensation component—one that is internally caused. But is there anything more to daydreaming than having sensations? It's not clear. But if daydreaming consists just of sensations, then some forms of thinking are just sensations.

Generally, of course, we do not think in visual imagery. Do thoughts devoid of visual imagery also include a sensation component? Often they do. Consider "mental chatter," the kind of thinking you probably do when washing the dishes by hand. When your mind is full of mental chatter, you are having a kind of internal conversation with yourself. This doesn't happen just when you wash dishes. A great deal of our thinking is internal conversation. Aren't the thoughts that occur during internal conversations usually also imagery—in this case, auditory imagery?

What, though, is an auditory image? Look at the next sentence and then repeat it silently to yourself:

"I am an auditory image."

What you heard in your mind was an auditory image. A great deal of your thinking occurs in the form of auditory images, which obviously include a sensation component—one that is internally, rather than externally, caused. But the experience of auditory imagery is similar to the experience of hearing. The main causal difference is that instead of coming from the outside, auditory images come from the inside. The main experiential difference is that auditory images are usually fainter than external sounds. Mental chatter, then, is also a sensation.

So thought often includes a sensation component. More than that, thought often *is* sensation. Isn't that odd? Thought and sensation seemed distinct enough a few paragraphs ago to make us wonder whether thought *ever* includes a sensation component. But now the relationship between thought and sensation seems so intimate that we may well wonder whether thought is anything *other* than sensation. We'll return to this question shortly.

We have seen that thought is often, perhaps always, just sensation. Let's see if sensation ever has a thought component. Wouldn't it be interesting to find that sensation often has a thought component? Wouldn't it be strange to discover that sensation just *is* thought? Wouldn't it be bizarre to realize that thought is sensation *and* sensation is thought?

When we considered your experience of the chair, your experience dissolved into two components: sensation and thought. We've now seen that thought often—perhaps always—is sensation. What, then, is sensation?

Consider again the example of pain. You just burned your hand on the stove. You feel pain in your finger. Pain is among our simplest sensations. Burning your hand on the stove is one of the simplest imaginable examples of pain.

Your finger hurts. This sensation has three distinct conceptual elements: "your," "finger," and "hurt." When your finger hurts, it is *your* finger that hurts, it is your *finger* that hurts, and it is your finger that *hurts*. Aren't "you," "finger," and "hurt" mental concepts rather than sensations? Aren't mental concepts a kind of thought? Let's find out.

Close your eyes and press your right index finger lightly against the cover of this book. What do you feel? Here are some possibilities:

1. You feel your finger press against *Wisdom without Answers*.
2. You feel your finger press against a book.
3. You feel your finger press against part of the surface of a book.
4. You feel pressure on the tip of your finger.
5. You feel pressure.
6. There is a feeling of pressure.
7. Pressure.
8. ...

You probably think you feel the first seven items on this list. If you press your finger against the cover of this book, you *should* feel them. But recall that there is a difference between what we actually experience and the interpretation we give to what we actually experience. Assume for the moment that you actually feel pressure on the tip of your finger—the fourth item on the list. Each of the first three descriptions is an interpretation over and above the mere fact that you feel pressure on the tip of your finger.

If what you actually feel is pressure on the tip of your finger, then isn't it your mind that interprets that pressure as part of the surface of a book? Then isn't it your mind that interprets that surface as "a book"? And then isn't it your mind that interprets that book as *Wisdom without Answers*?

Was it your finger that experienced the pressure as *Wisdom without Answers*, or was it your mind? Surely your finger didn't experience the pressure as *Wisdom without Answers*. Your finger doesn't know how to read! Your mind must have had the experience.

So it is with the other information in the first three items on the list. Your finger was affected by pressure, and your mind interpreted the pressure as a book or as the surface of a book. Aren't books and surfaces of books solid objects? How did your finger know that the pressure was a solid object? Obviously it didn't. Your mind knew the pressure was a solid object.

Therefore, the most you actually experienced independently of your mental contribution was pressure on the tip of your finger. But did you actually experience even that? How could you have? How could your finger know that the feeling of pressure was on the tip of your finger? Your finger doesn't have a brain. Your finger can't know anything without your mind's interpreting the pressure as pressure on the tip of your finger.

Once you delete the thought component from your experience, you realize that you did not actually feel the pressure *as pressure on the tip of your finger*. What then? Perhaps you just felt the pressure *as pressure*. Is that what you actually felt? Pressure? Is that what our tactile sensation of reality is—just pressure?

You did feel a sensation. The only sensation to be felt was pressure. It would seem to follow that you actually felt pressure. Of course you did, but the issue we are discussing is not whether you felt pressure. We are not disputing that you felt it. We are simply trying to separate the sensation component of that experience from the thought component to find out what it is about sensation, if anything, that puts us in touch with reality.

How did your finger know that the sensation was pressure? If your finger couldn't know that the pressure was on the tip of your finger, how could your finger know that the sensation it felt was pressure? Obviously your finger didn't know any such thing. Only minds know. Fingers supply data. Minds interpret data. "Pressure" is part of an interpretation.

What then was the actual, uninterpreted sensation? We have sunk to the bottom of the list, and we still don't know. Perhaps item eight on the list ("...") is what you actually felt. But what is item eight?

Consider again the example that launched our search: Your finger hurts. Does that sensation have a thought component? Yes. Does your finger know that it is *your* finger? No. Does your finger know that it is your *finger*? No. Does your finger know that the sensation it feels *hurts*? No. How could your finger possibly know any of these things? For that matter, does your finger even feel the sensation of pain?

Notice how closely our experiential account of the thought component of sensation corresponds to the scientific story of what happens when you touch a hot stove. According to the scientific story, the atoms are not white-hot; heat is merely the relative motion of atoms. The energy from this relative motion reaches out beyond the force of repulsion and affects the atoms of your finger. This energy initiates a chain of events that begins at the tip of your finger and ends in your brain. Your nerves send an electrical impulse to your brain. Your brain receives the electrical impulse and *interprets* this impulse as pain.

It may seem at first glance that your finger feels the sensation of pain, but—according to the scientific view—it is actually your brain that feels it. Your finger sends an electrochemical impulse. Your brain interprets this impulse as pain, and this interpretation involves thought.

We have already seen that thought often includes an element of sensation. Perhaps many thoughts are just sensations. Now we see that sensation often includes an element of thought. Perhaps many sensations are just thoughts. What then is thought? What is sensation? Could they be one and the same? The same *what?* Perhaps we have no better name for it than "experience." But what *is* experience?

When we looked at the chair, we saw that our experience dissolved into two fundamental components: sensation and thought. When we looked at each of these, we saw them reunite into one. For lack of a better word, we called this one thing "experience."

Experience is mind-dependent. But when we think of the chair that we experience, we think of the chair as something that exists "out there" independently of our minds. Experience is ephemeral—it comes and goes from moment to moment. But when we think of real objects like chairs, we think of them as being solid, permanent, and existing wholly independently of our minds.

We *seem* to experience the chair directly. Yet all we experience directly is our own experience. How, then, does our own experience, which is impermanent and insubstantial, appear to be permanent and substantial? In other words, how does the impermanent become permanent, the insubstantial solid, the mental concrete?

The two fundamental components of our experience—sensation and thought—are two different types of the same impermanent thing. Mixed together they create permanence. In other words, the relationship between sensing and thinking is a bit like the relationship between water and cement. Water, by itself, flows. Cement, by itself, crumbles. Water *and* cement, when mixed together, make concrete.

So it is with sensing and thinking. If you just look, or you just feel, or you just think, as we did in the case of our experience of the chair, you get something that flows or crumbles. If you look *and* think, or you feel *and* think, you get the experience of concrete objects—you get chairs.

Is the chair you experience—what you see and feel directly when you look at the chair you are sitting on—a real chair? We have seen that the chair you directly experience is a mixture of sensation and thought. Sensation and thought are both mind-dependent. Reality, we ordinarily believe, is something that exists independently of our minds. But if sensation—the one component of our experience that contains the least amount of mental contribution from us—can't get us all the way to the reality "out there," what can?

Perhaps thoughts can. After all, it's because we interpret the sensations of things like chairs and books that our experience seems to be of chairs and books rather than simply of pressure. Isn't it our thoughts that, mixed with sensation, lead us to experience reality as stable, permanent, and solid? But where do thoughts come from? Sensations of things like chairs, we think, are caused, ultimately, by the impact of the outside world on our sense organs. That gives sensation some sort of grounding in reality. What claim on reality, if any, do our thoughts have?

If our thoughts are based on nothing—if thought is just make-believe—then it's hard to see how thought can contribute to experience to get us all the way to reality. We need more than just make-believe stories. If thinking is going to provide the bridge between experience and reality, we need stories that we have some reason to believe are true. We have such stories: scientific theories.

Surely science, if anything, is our bridge from experience to reality. Scientific theories are complex thought-structures, but they are not just make-believe. They are thought-structures that we have good reason to believe are true. If science is the tree of knowledge, technology is the fruit. Science works. Make-believe doesn't.

Science may provide a bridge from experience to reality, but, if it does, it's not to the reality we directly experience. The chair of our direct experience is solid, colored, and stable. Recall, on the other hand, the scientific view of the chair, which we got to just by thinking. That chair is colorless, mostly empty space, and composed entirely of parts that are in constant, violent motion. What happened to the reality we directly experience?

According to science, the reality we directly experience is not reality but make-believe. If science is the bridge from experience to reality, then it's also the bridge from the familiar reality of our direct experience to a reality that is as alien to our ordinary view of ourselves and the world as the most bizarre science-fiction stories. Scientific theories do show us that we can have knowledge that goes way beyond direct experience. But, ironically, one of the things that it seems we then know is that the reality of our direct experience is mostly make-believe. Scientific theories don't pull us out of an abyss in which we are nobody floating freely nowhere; they push us in.

We've seen that our ordinary view of ourselves and the world is largely a product of thought. This ordinary view has the backing neither of science nor of direct experience. Is our ordinary view of reality, then, merely make-believe? That seems unlikely. After all, we've survived as a species precisely because we've been able to adapt to the world. If our ordinary view of reality were completely groundless, we wouldn't be here! But if our being here means we are somehow reliably connected to reality, what is the connection?

We went in search of reality and found several: the subjective reality of our sense experience; the partially subjective, partially objective reality of the world as we commonsensically view it; and the seemingly objective reality of the world as science views it. Are these three realities in competition with each other or merely different interpretions of the same thing—reality? But what is reality? Because the most obvious examples of real objects are the ones we directly experience—objects like tables and chairs—we turned to experience in the hope of finding out whether it gives us direct access to reality. The answer turned out to be another question: Which reality?

Experience, far from giving us direct access to reality, gives us direct access, so far as we know, only to ourselves. It is as if we who are nowhere and know nothing directly except our own experience end up building bridges that lead, ultimately, only back to ourselves.

CONSCIOUSNESS

9

We live in a reductionistic age. When we want to understand something scientifically, we explain it in terms of something else that is not that kind of thing. We drop down a level. For instance, we explain minds in terms of living bodies, living bodies in terms of non-living molecules, and so on.

This reductive strategy has been enormously successful; it has led to unparalleled refinements in our scientific understanding, so much so that our concept of rationality has been molded in its image. The reductive strategy has been so successful that the suggestion that it may have its limitations sounds unscientific and therefore irrational. Yet the very success of the reductive strategy increasingly forces us to face the issue of defining its limits. Two questions, in particular, are unavoidable: "Where, if anywhere, do the reductions end?" and "Have we lost anything along the way?"

The first question asks if the reductive process must somehow eventually bottom out. The second question asks if some things—even if they can be understood reductively—are nevertheless worth understanding on their own terms. The strategy of reductive understanding is a strategy of perpetually changing the topic. So the first question asks if we can continue to change the topic forever. The second asks if—even if we can—we always should.

The first question—Where do the reductions end?—has taken a curious turn in the twentieth century. The so-called soft sciences (such as psychology) are in the process of being reduced to the so-called hard sciences (such as chemistry and physics). The extent to which this reduction has been completed is usually considered the measure of scientific progress in the softer sciences. For instance, psychology has been substantially reduced to biology, which has been substantially reduced to chemistry, which has been substantially reduced to physics. Psychology begins by asking "What is mind?" Ultimately, physics answers the question in terms of matter and energy.

But what is physics reduced to? There is no science more basic than physics to which physics can be reduced. So it seems that physics is the end of the line, that physics has the last word, the ultimate answers.

One problem with this reassuring picture is that, during the twentieth century, physics hasn't been looking much like the end of the line. A surprising discovery in contemporary quantum mechanics—the most successful scientific theory ever developed—is that at the most fundamental level, mind comes back into the equation. Put in simplest terms:

We ask: What are minds?
We answer: living bodies of a certain kind.

We ask: What is a living body?
We answer: a collection of organic molecules.

We ask: What are organic molecules?
We answer: ultimately, inorganic molecules.

We ask: And what are they?
We answer: collections of atoms.

We ask: What are atoms?
We answer: electrons and neutrons and the like.

We ask: And what are they?
We answer: quarks.

We ask: What are quarks?
We answer: the result of *minds* at work collapsing waves of probability into actuality.

And so once more we ask: What are minds?

In other words, our minds have been reduced to biology, which has been reduced to chemistry, which has been reduced to physics, which has let mind in again through the back door. We began with the question "What are minds?" and we ended with the question "What are minds?" We turned away from consciousness in order to follow a reductive strategy that ultimately turned in on itself and led us back again to consciousness. This is Nature's little joke on the twentieth century: The reductive process bottoms out by turning back in on itself.

No one knows what this curious situation means for the reductive strategy and for the ideal of rationality that the strategy sustains. The issues here are so technical and the scientific developments so recent that they haven't yet been adequately discussed by philosophers or scientists. So it's too soon to say what this curious knowledge loop means. But it's not too soon to *ask* what it means. It's not too soon to wonder whether it will have profound implications for the future of the reductive strategy and the ideal of rationality that it sustains. There is a real possibility that it will.

Where then does the reductive strategy terminate? We start with mind, and one possibility is that we will end right where we began—with mind. Another is that we will end with some hitherto undiscovered ultimate constituent of everything. Another possibility—and one not to be dismissed, as we shall see in the next chapter—is that we will end, literally, with nothing.

What of the second question: Have we lost anything along the way? If there is something that is worth understanding on its own terms and not just reductively, then we *have* lost something. The obvious candidate for what we've lost is the mind in its subjective mode—that is, consciousness or experience. We may be forced ultimately to understand consciousness nonreductively or not at all. But even if we're not forced to understand consciousness nonreductively, that is, experientially, we may derive great benefits from understanding it experientially. When we understand ourselves scientifically, we understand ourselves from the outside, as just another object in nature. When we understand ourselves experientially, we understand ourselves from the inside, as a subject.

What's the difference? The difference is in the *kind* of understanding that results. The difference is between knowing *about* something and simply knowing that thing. When we understand, say, love or anxiety scientifically we know *about* them. When we understand them experientially we know *them*. We can have the first kind of knowledge even if we've never been in love or experienced anxiety. We can have the second kind of knowledge only if we've had the experience.

A blind person can understand the science of color. Only a person with sight knows what it's like to experience the colors of a sunset. The first kind of knowledge is scientifically rich. The second is experientially rich. They are not in competition with each other. Both sorts of knowledge are essential if we are to understand ourselves and the world fully.

We know that scientific knowledge requires special training. But we tend to assume that experiential knowledge just happens. In a sense it does; in the normal course of living we learn more about life than about physics. But we may not learn much about life. Having an experience and understanding that experience are different things. One does not necessarily lead to the other.

We've already seen where we will end up if we carry the reductive strategy to its limit: with mind or with some hitherto undiscovered something or with nothing. This last possibility—that ultimately we come face to face with nothing—has already been glimpsed on the horizons of science: Cosmologists trying to understand the origin of the universe have had to face the strange possibility that the universe—which exists nowhere and never happens—came from nothing.

COSMOS

10

Imagine nothingness: No planets or stars. No people. No thoughts or feelings. No matter or energy. No space. No time. Not even emptiness, for emptiness implies a container.

This may be difficult to imagine. So let's start with emptiness. Look around you. You're looking at mostly empty space. All those apparently solid objects are merely configurations of atoms, which are themselves mostly empty space. Furthermore, "solid" objects are scarce. The universe contains much more empty space than matter. In the vast distances between stars there is on the average only one subatomic particle per square kilometer of space.

So the universe has very little matter; in fact, the ratio of matter to empty space is about one part to a billion. If we applied U.S. government standards for determining the amount of salt in food to the question of how much matter there is in the universe, we would conclude that the universe is matter-free.

Thus you don't have to do much to imagine emptiness. Emptiness surrounded by emptiness is what we are. Emptiness is close to nothing. So if you want to get an approximate idea of what nothing looks like, just look around! Look toward the heavens. Look around your living room. Look in a mirror. *Everything you see is almost nothing.*

Thus the universe, which is nowhere and never, is mostly empty space, and empty space is close to nothing. Yet *something* exists. We might not know, ultimately, what it is, but it's not just nothing.

Why isn't there *just* nothing? Why does anything at all exist rather than nothing? One old answer is that God created the universe. God, we are told, has always existed without beginning or end and is responsible for the existence of both space and time—but is not anywhere *in* space and time.

If God created the universe, then the universe exists because God created it. But God is not nothing; God, too—whether God is a

70

thing or not—is something. So the old religious answer merely pushes the question of why there is something rather than nothing one step further back. It does not answer the question. For now we must ask: Why God rather than nothing?

To answer the question of why anything at all exists rather than nothing, religion would also have to explain why God exists. Can religion explain why God exists? One possibility is that God has always existed. Suppose that's true. Would that explain why something—in this case God—exists rather than nothing?

No. The claim that God has always existed tells us *that* God has always existed but not *why* God has always existed. To answer the question of why something exists rather than nothing, religion would have to explain why God exists.

Some theologians believe the question of why God exists doesn't have an answer, or that, if it does have an answer, we can't know what it is. They believe God is beyond reason. These theologians, therefore, would have to concede that ultimately there is no knowable answer to the question of why something exists rather than nothing.

Other theologians believe that there is a reason why God exists: It is not possible for God *not* to exist. In their view, the very nature of God ensures that God exists. God exists because God has to exist. God exists necessarily. These theologians claim that the universe— unlike God—does not exist necessarily. They claim that if it weren't for an external cause—God—the universe would not exist. God "explains" the universe. But what explains God? God explains God. God explains everything—even God. So, why does something exist rather than nothing? In this view, the universe exists because God created it and God exists because God exists necessarily.

This religious answer is not the only answer to the question of why something exists rather than nothing. Science has several answers—some old, some new. The oldest scientific answer is as old as the oldest religious answer. It says that the reason the universe exists is that the universe has always existed. The universe is infinitely old.

This, however, does not answer our question. This answer didn't work for religion, and it doesn't work for science either. *That* the universe has always existed doesn't explain *why* the universe has always existed.

Could science explain why the universe has always existed? Classical physicists claimed that matter can be neither created nor destroyed. Because the universe exists now, they argued, it must have existed always. Thus something exists because something—in this case the whole universe—exists necessarily.

Is this a better answer than the religious answer? Yes. Everyone agrees that the universe exists. We can see much of it. That God exists is both questionable and controversial. Few of us claim to have seen God. So if we must say that something exists necessarily in order to explain why the universe exists rather than nothing, why not just say that what exists necessarily is the universe itself? What's simpler—the idea of a necessarily existent universe or the idea of a universe *plus* a necessarily existent spiritual being?

However, one of the most startling scientific developments of all time is the recent theory that the universe has not always existed, that it is *not* infinitely old. The latest evidence suggests that the universe had a definite beginning at least fifteen billion years ago.

In the beginning was the Big Bang. Our universe exploded into existence as an infinitesimally small point and began expanding at the speed of light. Everything—not just the matter that makes up you and all the people and objects that have ever existed, but all the matter of every planet and every star in the billions of galaxies—fit into a tiny space smaller than a thimble. There was very little empty space then. But there was the same amount of stuff there is now; it just wasn't as dispersed. Can this amazing Big Bang theory explain why something exists rather than nothing?

No. The Big Bang theory tells us where the universe came from— an infinitesimally small point. But the Big Bang theory doesn't tell us *why* the Big Bang occurred; it doesn't explain the Big Bang. Thus the Big Bang theory doesn't explain why something—in this case the universe—exists rather than nothing.

Perhaps if we knew why the Big Bang occurred, we would know why something exists rather than nothing. So, why did the Big Bang occur?

One theory is that the Big Bang happened as a result of a previous universe collapsing into a Big Crunch. The momentum from this Big Crunch produced our Big Bang. When our universe runs its course, it will also collapse into another big crunch, which will in turn produce the next big bang and thus the next universe, and so on. Suppose that this theory of cyclical universes is true. Would it answer our question?

No. The cyclical universe theory merely postpones the question. The birth of our universe is explained by the death of a previous universe, the birth of which is in turn explained by the death of another universe, and so on. This is a bit like paying your American Express bill with another credit card and then paying the second bill with a third credit card, and so on. You merely postpone paying your bill. If you actually tried this, you'd get arrested for fraud.

But what if you had an infinite number of credit cards? Then you might be able to prolong the billing process forever. Isn't the cyclical universe theory a little like having an infinite number of credit cards? If you had an infinite number of credit cards, you could charge any particular bill, but you'd never actually pay up. You'd merely prolong the billing process—forever. Similarly, the cyclical universe theory could account for the existence of this or any particular universe. But it never answers the question of why something—in this case the whole chain of cyclical universes—exists rather than nothing. It merely prolongs the questioning process forever.

Suppose the cyclical universe theory is wrong; suppose there *was* a first moment. Then the Big Bang was the moment of creation. Creation has traditionally been considered a religious issue, forever beyond the realm of science. Surprisingly, however, some contemporary scientists have ventured even beyond the first moment of creation, beyond the Big Bang. To them, the idea that nothing preceded our universe is not so much a problem as a solution. Neither the Big Crunch nor anything else created our universe. Rather, our universe was created literally from nothing.

Genesis, then, goes like this: In the beginning there was nothing. No God. No space. No time. No matter. No energy. Then the Big Bang: Time, space, and energy exploded into existence out of nowhere and the universe was born.

But how can this "creation of the universe from nothing" scenario explain why something exists rather than nothing? One explanation is that the universe exists because nothingness is unstable. Why the Big Bang? Why something rather than nothing? Because nothingness is unstable. As one physicist recently remarked, "They say there's no such thing as a free lunch. The universe, however, is a free lunch."

An unstable nothingness? It sounds as if "nothingness" is a sort of thing—a mysterious energy-free, space-free, time-free, matter-free object that happened to be unstable. But nothingness is *not* a thing. Nothingness is just nothing.

Here is the way the "creation of the universe from nothing" scenario tries to explain why something exists rather than nothing:

Something—in this case the universe—exists because nothingness, being unstable, degenerated into something. Nothingness, one could say, "nothinged itself." This answer, however, raises yet another question: Why is nothingness unstable? For if nothingness were stable, there would still be just nothing.

Perhaps there is no reason why nothingness is unstable. Then we could not explain fully why something exists rather than nothing. We would merely have pushed the mystery of existence one step further back.

But perhaps nothingness is unstable for a reason. What could this reason be? It couldn't be that anything *makes* nothingness unstable. There is nothing to make nothingness unstable! So if nothingness is unstable for a reason, it must be that nothingness is unstable by its very nature.

Would this explain why something exists rather than nothing? It might. Two problems remain, however. First, how could nothingness have a nature? If nothingness has a nature, aren't we mislabeling it when we call it *nothingness?* Isn't it then something? And if nothingness is something, then we've merely pushed our question one step further back. We haven't explained why something exists rather than nothing.

Second, why does nothingness have the nature it has rather than some other nature? If there is no reason why nothingness has the nature it has, then the theory can't fully explain why something exists rather than nothing. This theory—that the universe exists because nothingness is unstable by its very nature—would explain fully why something (in this case, the universe) exists only if there was some reason why nothingness has the nature it has.

There is only one way to explain why nothingness has the nature it has. Since nothingness is just nothing, the explanation would have to be that nothingness itself explains its own instability. There's nothing else to explain it.

But how could nothingness explain its own instability? If nothingness *just happens* to be unstable, it can't explain it. If, on the other hand, nothingness *has* to be unstable, nothingness could explain its own instability. The explanation would be this: Nothingness is unstable because nothingness is unstable *necessarily.*

Suppose then that nothingness is unstable necessarily. It would follow that something exists necessarily. Then something exists rather than nothing because there *has* to be something. But why *this* something? Why a universe? More importantly, why *this* universe rather than, say, a chaotic universe without any life forms? Either there is no explanation of why this universe exists, or else nothingness produced this universe necessarily.

How could nothingness produce the very universe that exists right now—our universe—necessarily? One possibility is based on the idea that we—the questioners—can exist only in a well-ordered universe such as the one that exists right now. When nothingness degenerates into chaotic universes, we're not there to ask about it. That's why the universe in question—our universe—has to be well ordered. Any universe with questioners in it will be well ordered because that is a requirement for there being any questioners.

Is this so-called Anthropic Principle a good explanation? One problem is that it requires the idea that what comes later can explain what came earlier. Physicists have indeed shown how reverse causation can work in some cases. But whether our presence in the universe can explain why this universe exists remains to be seen. The problem is that the *most* our presence in the universe could explain is the existence of *some* well-ordered universe—one sufficiently ordered and stable to produce questioners. It couldn't explain why *this* universe exists rather than some other, comparably well-ordered universe. Is there any way that the idea of an unstable nothingness could explain the existence of *this* universe?

Yes. The explanation of *this* universe coming into being from nothingness must be that nothingness generated this universe necessarily. In other words, the ultimate explanation of why something exists rather than nothing—if there is an ultimate explanation—must be that this universe exists necessarily.

Suppose, for example, that nothingness did not generate this universe necessarily. Then what could explain this universe? There would be no explanation. So, if there is an explanation, it must be that nothingness generated this universe necessarily. Ultimately, then, in this view, *this* universe *must* exist. *This* universe exists necessarily.

Many philosophers past and present think that the question of why something exists rather than nothing is unscientific. Some have claimed that the question is meaningless because it could never, even in principle, be answered. Others have claimed that the question lies in the realm of metaphysics, forever beyond the reach of science.

Science has proven these philosophers wrong. Modern science has not ignored the question of why something exists rather than nothing. For the first time ever, the question has a possible scientific answer based on the idea that because nothingness is necessarily unstable, this universe necessarily exists. Why is there something rather than nothing? Ultimately, because something—this universe—necessarily exists.

Sound familiar? It should. The scientific answer is remarkably like the religious answer. Why does something exist rather than nothing? Because something exists necessarily. For religion, God exists necessarily. For science, the universe exists necessarily.

Science and religion both offer a choice. Either there is no reason why something exists rather than nothing, or else something—either God or the universe—exists necessarily. According to religion, God gives rise to the universe. According to modern science, nothingness gives rise to the universe. According to religion, God gives rise to space and time and matter and energy. According to modern science, nothingness gives rise to space and time and matter and energy.

Isn't it odd that what religion understands by *God* is very close to what modern science understands by *nothingness?* Neither God nor nothingness exists in space or time; both give rise to the universe of space, time, energy, and matter.

What then is the difference between God and nothingness? One difference is that whereas God is essentially stable, nothingness is essentially unstable. This seemingly important difference between God and nothingness masks a genuinely important similarity. Neither God nor nothingness rests content with itself as it is (or is not). God does not just stay God; God gives rise to something. Nothingness does not just stay nothing; it gives rise to something. Both God and nothingness give rise to the *same* something—this universe.

Not remaining the same. Not resting content. Do we have a name for this condition? Theologians call it God. Scientists call it nothingness. If we didn't know better, we'd call it *craving*.

EATH

When you die you won't vanish into nothing. In one form or another, every bit of material of every person who has ever lived still exists. The same will be true of you. The atoms of your body won't vanish. They will be absorbed by soil, plants, animals, and people.

Every living thing feeds on death. We humans feed on animals and plants. Animals feed either on other animals or on plants. Plants feed on the soil. But all animals and plants, when they die, return to the soil. Death nourishes the soil. Life recycles itself through death.

So, in a sense, you will continue to exist after your bodily death. But this is little consolation. You want *you*—not the atoms of your body, but *you*—to survive the decomposition of your body.

If you survive the decomposition of your present physical body, you must survive as something other than your present body—perhaps a soul. But what is a soul, and do you have one?

Souls are not bodies or memories or beliefs or character traits or temperamental dispositions. If souls were bodies, they would decompose when we die. If souls were memories, they would diminish as we got older. If souls were beliefs, they would change from day to day. If souls were character traits or temperamental dispositions, a lobotomy could destroy them.

Traditionally, souls are thought of as "spiritual" substances that *have* memories, beliefs, character traits, and so on; souls are not these phenomena themselves but, rather, spiritual things that *have* them. Today we believe that it is the body—more specifically, the brain— that has memories, beliefs, character traits, and so on. We can explain the functioning of the body by appeal, ultimately, to the behavior of atoms.

People used to appeal to souls to explain the functioning of the body because they thought a spiritual substance was needed to animate matter. Today we understand matter to be energy, a universal physical substance—"mass-energy"—that can account fully, without appeal to souls, for all the properties of living things.

Contemporary psychology has shown us that memories and beliefs and character traits grow out of experience. Biology has shown us that bodies, and even some temperamental dispositions, grow out of genes. Physics has shown why atoms form the sorts of structures that give rise to biology and psychology. What, then, is left for a soul to do? Apparently nothing—at least not while the body is alive. After the body dies, however, the soul supposedly takes over the job previously done by physical atoms. Souls, then, are like spiritual atoms. It takes only one soul—one spiritual atom—to do the job of lots of material atoms.

Souls and physical atoms are both invisible to the naked eye. However, whereas physical atoms are visible through electron microscopes, souls are not visible at all. It is not just that we need better microscopes to see souls. Even with better microscopes we couldn't see them. Even if we had devices through which we saw colors or shapes surrounding bodies, we'd be looking at colors and shapes, which are physical phenomena, not souls. We could *never* see souls, even in principle, through any physical device, because souls are not physical phenomena.

Are souls a possible answer to whether there is life after death? Perhaps. But they are a redundant answer. Bodies are composed of atoms. Souls are a kind of spiritual atom. If you were dissatisfied with the answer that you survive your bodily death because the atoms of your body survive, then why be satisfied with the answer that you survive because your spiritual atom survives? Billions of nearly indestructible but verifiable physical atoms from your body survive your bodily death, and you are dissatisfied. One spiritual atom—which could never, even in principle, be observed—survives, and you are satisfied. Why?

Isn't it because you think that physical atoms could not possibly sustain your psychology after the death of your physical body, whereas your spiritual atom could? But why assume this? Perhaps your physical atoms, even as dispersed as they would be after death, could sustain your psychology. There is no evidence that they could; but it is *possible* that they could. Which is more bizarre—the idea that your psychology is somehow preserved by physical atoms, which are known to exist, or that your psychology is somehow preserved by a nonphysical, spiritual atom, which is not known to exist and which cannot even in principle be observed?

Perhaps we have gone too fast. Perhaps there is evidence that souls exist. After all, isn't there evidence that some people have survived their bodily deaths?

Right now we are not questioning whether there is evidence that some people have survived their bodily deaths. Even if there were such evidence, our point is simply that there is no reason to believe that souls have anything to do with it because there is no evidence that souls exist. More than that, there *couldn't* be any evidence that souls exist. Yet—surprisingly—there still might be evidence that some people have survived their bodily deaths.

So, let's turn to the question of whether there is any evidence that some people have survived their bodily deaths. After all, what difference does it make if you survive your bodily death as a soul or if you survive in some physical way? The mode of transportation is a mere detail. Survival, on the other hand, is a matter of life and death.

Everyone has heard stories about life after death. There are the old-fashioned religious stories. There are the new-fashioned psychic phenomena stories. Is there any truth to any of them?

The religious stories may or may not be true. But this much is certain: If we are to accept religious stories as evidence, we will end up with contradictory evidence. There are many different religious stories from many different religious traditions, and these stories contradict each other. Some say that after death we immediately continue existing in another world. Others say that after death we cease to exist until the final day of this world. Some say we leave Earth forever and go to either a heaven or a hell. Others say we are reborn on Earth again and again and again. Some say we survive as material beings. Others say we survive as spiritual beings. Some say we survive as personal beings. Others say that, eventually, we lose our individuality completely and merge with the cosmos. Some say we spend eternity sitting at the feet of God. Others say we are God. We could go on for another twenty pages or so, but our point should be obvious: Religious *stories* cancel each other out. Perhaps that's why, throughout history, religious *people* have tried to cancel each other out!

One of the religious stories, however, may still be true. Even if one of them is true, however, none of them is *evidence* that anyone has ever survived bodily death. For every story there is another equally credible story that contradicts it, and contradictory evidence is self-defeating—it is like having no evidence at all. If there is evidence for life after death, it must be found elsewhere.

But couldn't someone argue that, *collectively*, the religious stories provide good evidence for life after death? After all, the diverse religious stories do agree on one thing: survival. They differ merely on the details. So aren't they good evidence for survival? No. Agreement in this case merely shows that a common theme can be found in almost all the world's religions. Psychology can easily explain this common theme. One psychology text puts it like this: "Stimuli pertaining to death can be regarded as a subset of the larger set of stimuli that elicit avoidance or distress responses." We would put it like this: People fear death. They fear it not just here and there, or once in a while, but everywhere and always. Fearing death, people have a strong motive to deny it.

Someone might not agree with this explanation of why religious stories tend to promote the idea of survival of bodily death. Someone might think that the religious stories suggest a truth about survival, not a truth about human psychology. But the explanation in terms of human psychology is not only simpler, it is testable. The explanation in terms of survival, on the other hand, is speculative at best, more complex, and impossible to test either directly or indirectly. Thus believing in survival on the basis of religious stories isn't belief based on good evidence. It is belief based on faith. And it is based not *just* on faith, but on faith that goes *contrary* to the best available evidence.

So much for the old-fashioned religious stories. What about the new-fashioned psychic phenomena stories? These stories vary a lot in specifics, but they can all be broadly categorized in terms of the three basic types of phenomena they describe: remembrances of past lives, apparitions of dead people, and experiences of dying and coming back. Because each type of phenomenon includes many subcategories, the result may seem a bewildering array of different sorts of arguments. There is, however, a simple common core to all arguments based on such evidence. They can all be understood as having two premises and a conclusion. The first premise is that some unusual phenomenon has happened—an apparition, a memory of a past life, a strange experience, and so on. The second (usually implicit) premise is that *the best explanation* of the unusual phenomenon implies that someone has survived bodily death. The conclusion is that someone *has* survived bodily death.

A problem with all such arguments is that there is never just one possible explanation of the report of the unusual phenomenon, but four: (1) fraud, (2) unknown but ordinary circumstances, (3) some psychic phenomenon like ESP, and (4) survival of bodily death. For instance, if someone under hypnosis claims to remember doing things he or she did in some previous life, it might be a trick—fraud. Or the person might be apparently remembering information learned in some ordinary—but forgotten—way. Or the person might have ESP; that is, he or she might be not remembering a previous life but picking up the information in some other extraordinary (but eventually explicable) way. Or the person might actually be remembering a previous life. These four possibilities have to be weighed against each other. For the evidence to show that people survive their bodily deaths, the evidence must favor the survival hypothesis—the fourth possible explanation—more than the other three.

People who consider reports of such unusual phenomena are often unaware that there are four possible explanations. They frequently assume there is just one explanation—survival. Furthermore, they are often unaware that to make the case, on the basis of evidence, that the particular explanation they favor is the most probable one, they must *show* that their favorite explanation is better supported by evidence than are the other three. Therefore, given these four possible explanations of any unusual phenomenon, do such phenomena provide adequate evidence for survival of bodily death? To provide such evidence, the survival hypothesis would at least sometimes have to be the most likely explanation. Is it ever?

To decide, we must consider all relevant information, for instance, that the person relating the incident often stands to gain something—money, prestige, credibility—and thus often has a motive for fraudulent behavior. If the person does have a motive for fraudulent behavior, this doesn't prove that the person is a fraud. But it counts in favor of the fraud explanation and against the other three possible explanations. Thus, in the end, we have to ask ourselves which is the more plausible explanation: that the person is pulling a clever trick or that someone has actually survived bodily death.

Suppose, however, that you have information that counts against fraud; for instance, the person apparently remembering a previous life is *you*. In that case, is survival of bodily death the most plausible explanation?

Not necessarily. The survival hypothesis still has to be weighed against the other two explanations. One possibility is that your memory was stimulated by some information you acquired in a normal way. For instance, you read as a child about a place you've never been to and now you think you remember having actually been there. Which is more plausible—that some such unusual turn of events resulted in your making a mistake or that you are actually remembering a previous life? The same applies to the additional possibility of self-deception. What could be the motive for self-deception? Fear could, or the desire to reduce anxiety about death.

The obvious first step is to do more checking. There is always the chance that the phenomenon in question, no matter how strange, will have an ordinary explanation. There is also the chance it won't. To support the survival hypothesis, however, it is not enough that *at present* there is no known explanation of the phenomenon. The chance that there is some as yet unknown, but ordinary, explanation must be weighed against the likelihood of the survival explanation. Thus, barring further information, in the case we've been considering, which is the *likelier* explanation: that your apparent remembering of a previous life has some ordinary explanation, or that you actually remember your previous life?

Suppose further information makes it unlikely that there is an ordinary explanation of your apparent remembering. Suppose, for instance, that you are a four-year-old who has just identified a perfect stranger as the man who murdered you ten years ago. Furthermore, you give his name and the location of the murder, and you relate evidence that, when checked, is found to be true and is sufficient to convict him. You seem to remember all the details as if they happened to you. Would this be adequate to show that you actually survived your bodily death?

No. The survival hypothesis has now to be weighed against the ESP explanation. For the survival hypothesis to win, however, there must be more evidence for it than for the ESP explanation. This, ultimately, is where the survival hypothesis always faces its most severe challenge.

There might someday be evidence that survival of bodily death is a more likely explanation of the new-fashioned psychic phenomena stories than is the ESP explanation. But it is hard to see how that could be the case today. If we assume that ESP actually exists, we have almost no idea how it works. Thus we have little reason for concluding that ESP could *not* produce the unusual phenomena. Out-of-body experiences, near-death experiences, apparitions, and so on are—today at least—as well explained by ESP as they are by the survival hypothesis.

This is not to say that the ESP explanation is necessarily better than the survival hypothesis or that either is necessarily better than one of the first two alternatives. Our point is that it is difficult to make the case that the evidence that now exists favors the survival hypothesis over *all other* possible explanations. And that is what the survival hypothesis would have to do to emerge as the most likely explanation. Thus no evidence that now exists from new-fashioned psychic phenomena stories provides good evidence for believing that people survive their bodily deaths.

So much for both the new-fashioned psychic phenomena stories and the old-fashioned religious stories. Where does this leave us? It leaves us where we began: with life *before* death. If you find this depressing, recall that the parts out of which you are composed, both physical and mental, are constantly "dying" and being replaced. Our ordinary, day-to-day lives *are* a kind of life after death! So we do, after all, get life after death. We get it where we never expected it: *Here.*

Meaning

12

Why are we here? What's it all about? Is there some purpose or meaning to life?

At one time or another, everyone asks such questions. As children and as old people, especially, we wonder: Why? What does it all mean? Most of the rest of the time, we're so busy trying to be successful we don't worry about meaning. But even then, in the back of our minds, we may still wonder. And when we do, what is it we really want to know?

Suppose you're at a party. You love being with the people there; they love having you there. The music is terrific, the food and drinks are delicious, and everything is paid for. No one has to go anywhere, do anything, be any particular way. Everyone is having a wonderful time. Suddenly someone turns to you and asks, "Why are we here? What is the meaning of this party?" You'd probably consider the question irrelevant. Suppose, on the other hand, the party is terrible. Then you might think the question has a point.

So also with the question "What is the meaning of life?" When life is wonderful, we don't ask what it means—we're too busy enjoying it. When life is a painful struggle, the question forces itself upon us not so much because we want to answer the question of the meaning of life but, rather, because we want to end our struggle. We don't then care about solving the problem of the *meaning* of life. We care about solving the problem of *life*.

Everyone wants to have a good time. And it seems everyone has a recipe. Yet nearly everyone is struggling. There must be something wrong with the recipes.

Nearly everyone *is* struggling, not only in the poorest parts of the world, but everywhere. Poor people struggle just to survive, but even affluent people struggle. Everywhere, nearly everyone is *always* struggling. Why? What can we do about our struggles? Isn't that

84

what we usually want to know when the question of the meaning of life bothers us?

Theoretical answers may be of theoretical interest. But even after all the philosophy books, novels, songs, poems, and movies, people are still struggling. Lots of answers to the meaning of life have been given—some serious, some funny, some clever, some stupid—but none of them have ended the struggle. Why?

The problem is not that we don't have enough answers to the question "What is the meaning of life?" (we have too many) but that our lives are a struggle. It's not necessarily that the answers are wrong (though since most of them are incompatible with each other most of them must be wrong) but that the answers don't end the struggle. Why is that?

The problem is with the answers. And there are two problems. The first is that almost all the answers are answers to the wrong question. They attempt to tell us the meaning of life when what we need is a solution to life's struggles. The second problem with the answers is *that they are answers.* For even if we had the answer to the question of why life is such a struggle, this would not by itself end life's struggles. Knowing *why* life is such a struggle might change things a great deal. But answers can't be the answer. To see why, we shall first have to answer the question of why life is a struggle. Until we have that answer, it will always be tempting to suppose that if only we did have the answer, it would end life's struggles.

So why is life such a struggle? What's the answer?

Everyone knows it takes two to have a fight. You can't be involved in a struggle unless someone or something is resisting. The resistance may come from the outside or from the inside—you may be divided from someone else, or from your environment, or from yourself. Without division there can be no resistance. Without resistance there can be no struggle.

So the way to stop struggling is to end the fragmentation that leads to resistance. The problem is that we don't want to stop struggling at the cost of being dominated. If we drop all resistance, someone else is sure to dominate us. But even people whom no one is trying to dominate, even those in control, are struggling. In some places in the world, and at some times, struggle comes from the outside. But at all places in the world, and at all times, struggle comes from the inside.

What is *your* internal struggle? You're reading this book. Chances are no one is trying to shoot you. Chances are, though, that you are bothered by some internal struggle. How can you live without internal struggle? When you're bothered by questions about the meaning of life, isn't that what you usually want to know?

External and internal struggle both can be stopped in the same way: Drop all resistance. The problem with this answer in the case of external struggle is that we're afraid of being dominated. But no such problem exists in the case of internal struggle. In fact, just the opposite is the case. The reason you're bothered by internal struggle in the first place is that you're trying to dominate yourself—one part of you is trying to dominate another part of you.

Consider the simplest possible example of internal struggle. Suppose you drink too much alcohol and it bothers you. Part of you wants to continue. Another part of you wants to quit. If *all* of you wants to continue drinking, there is no struggle; you just drink. If *all* of you wants to quit, there is no struggle; you just quit. The problem is how to decide which part of yourself should prevail—in this case, the drinker or the nondrinker—and then how to get the other part to stop resisting.

Almost all internal struggle follows the same pattern. There is what you *are* and there is what you think you *should* be. That is the essence of most internal conflict. (That's why many of the answers to the meaning of life, such as religious answers, merely fuel the problem of internal struggle: They widen the gap by distancing you from yourself—that is, by creating within you an idealization of you.) So which part should prevail—the actual you, who exists right now, or the ideal you, who might exist sometime in the future?

You might end your internal struggle in two ways: by eventually becoming the ideal you or by accepting yourself exactly as you are right now and dropping all notions of how you should be. The first way, you continue struggling with yourself in the hope your struggle will end some day. The second way, you stop struggling right away.

It is difficult to drop being the way we are. It is easier to drop all notions of how we should be. We might eventually be able to change the way we are, but "trying to change" is a sure formula for perpetuating the struggle.

So, in the simple case of the drinker versus the nondrinker, who wins? If the source of the drinker's conflict is a tension between who the drinker is and who the drinker would like to be, then for the time being, the drinker wins. That doesn't necessarily mean that the drinker will always be a drinker. Maybe—but not necessarily. Accepting the fact of being a drinker, accepting it without condition that you change, may, as we shall see, be an effective way to become a nondrinker. The evolution might not take place, but there is a chance it will. One thing is certain: If the evolution does take place, it will be effortless.

But what if the drinker is addicted? Won't surrendering all resistance mean oblivion and death? Perhaps. But continuing to struggle with addiction might also mean oblivion and death—after great effort and pain! If one must drink oneself to death, isn't it better to do it effortlessly rather than with great struggle and pain?

We are all addicted to one thing or another. Accepting ourselves as we are without the condition that we change might give us insight into the causes of our addictions. For instance, one major reason people enjoy alcohol is that it makes them less inhibited. But why are they inhibited in the first place? Isn't that kind of inhibition often the result of their own resistance against what they themselves really are? Alcohol takes away inhibition and allows the inhibited part to come out. Often, self-destructive behavior is the inhibited part of you, ordinarily repressed by the ideal you, finally exerting itself and saying, "If you don't let me out, I'll kill you!" So the drinker who allows self-acceptance might become less inhibited—even without alcohol—and, in turn, might be less prone to drug abuse.

But if we all cease struggling, won't we just lie around all day? What will move us to act? Perhaps nothing. We might lie around all day. But one thing that *could* move us to act is love of some activity. We don't need to be coerced into doing what we love to do.

So, whatever your struggle, the way out of that struggle might be to accept yourself as you are without the condition that you change. The alternative would be to keep struggling. That's the alternative most of us take because, deep down, we believe that struggle is the price we must pay for success. Without struggle, we think, we could never go from being what we are now to being the successful person we would someday like to be. But there is something suspicious about this strategy: Nearly everyone is struggling, yet few are successful.

Ordinarily, when we call someone successful, we're talking about career. That is only one kind of success. You can also be successful as a person—for instance, by being happy and by contributing to the

happiness of others. Professional and personal success don't necessarily go together. We all know people who are successful in their careers but failures as persons and many people who have failed in
their careers but are successful as persons. Struggling does not ensure
either kind of success. Does anything?

There may be no single key to having a successful career. But
there is a common element: The farmer who becomes a successful
farmer, the doctor who becomes a successful doctor, the playwright
who becomes a successful playwright, and so on, all become successful by pleasing others. To make money, for instance, you have to
sell something or provide a service that someone else wants to pay
for. Somewhere down the line, all types of professional success require pleasing others.

What, then, of being successful as a person? Oddly enough, here
too success usually requires pleasing others. Being happy at work,
being a good friend, a good parent, a good lover, and so on, all ultimately involve pleasing others.

Few of us are hermits. Even pleasing ourselves usually involves
pleasing others. We may like to think of ourselves as individualists.
The truth is that being successful as a person—being happy and contributing to the happiness of others—almost always involves pleasing others. So a common element to both professional and personal
success is pleasing others.

Instinctively we already know this. But we tend to view ourselves through the lens of an idealized self-image that exaggerates
the extent of our independence. We don't like to admit the extent to
which we depend, even for our happiness, on the approval of others.
We like to think that we don't care what people think of us. The truth
is, we do care. This creates a tension within us, an internal struggle
between the part of us that wants approval and the part that wants
independence from the need for approval.

There is an ironic twist to this tension within us. We think the
way to independence is through success. But the way to success is almost always through the approval of others. The student, the archi-
tect, the actor, the grocer, and the football player are all dependent
on the approval of bosses, clients, fans, and so on, to gain greater independence from their need for approval.

We're all in the same boat. For instance, the authors of this book
think that if this book is a great success, they will become more independent and will be better able to go where they want, do what

they want, write what they want, and so on, without having to worry about what others think. The authors want to free themselves from the need for approval. How are they going to do it? Like everyone else, if they gain their independence from the need for the approval of others, it will be by gaining the approval of others.

This irony about success cuts deeply into all of our lives. Consider, for example, the way power is distributed in a romantic relationship. The one who is more powerful is the one who is less dependent on the other. How do you get less dependent? Usually by having more choice as to whom you are with. The better you are at pleasing others, all else being equal, the more choice you have as to whom you are with. The more choice you have, the more independent you are. So even in romantic relationships the way to independence is through pleasing others. Ironically, the way to independence is through dependence.

It may seem, then, from what we've just said that seeking approval is the key to success. If success is impossible without approval, then the way to success would seem to be to aim directly for it. That is what most of us do.

This strategy can't be completely wrong. After all, we've just seen that the approval of others is necessary for success. For instance, most students want to get good grades. That is their criterion of success. Students instinctively know that the surest way to get good grades is to get approval from their teachers by agreeing with them. This strategy works—but only to a point. It often, but not always, ensures that the student gets good grades. But merely getting good grades is a mediocre level of success. As every good teacher knows, those students who reach a high level of success in school—academic excellence—develop the capacity for *independent* thought. Getting good grades, on the other hand, usually doesn't ensure that a student has developed this capacity.

Students who agree with their teachers tend to get good grades partly because imitating their teachers' views on the material they are studying is the first level of connecting to that material. The best students then go on to challenge the opinions of their teachers in creative ways. The best students, once they have achieved the initial connection between themselves and the subject matter through imitating the teacher, then go on to connect to the subject matter directly. This requires taking risks—in particular, risking the disapproval of their teachers. Ultimately, what must matter most to these students is not the connection between themselves and their teachers but the connection between themselves and the truth about their subject matter.

Seeking approval is the first step to success. But it only goes so far. In the end, it is even limiting. If you want to reach higher levels of success, you must win approval not by seeking it but rather by achieving some level of excellence through connecting directly to the activity you are involved in. The twist is that achieving excellence through directly connecting to an activity can never be attained so long as one is primarily concerned with seeking approval. To attain success in its fullest form one must drop the quest for approval.

People tend to think success has something to do with pleasing others because that is itself an indirect way of connecting with an activity. But pleasing others is also a byproduct of connecting directly with an activity. In the end, what matters most is not approval but connecting directly with an activity, for that is the way to attain a high level of success. For instance, you might get a promotion by pleasing your boss, a job as an actor by pleasing a director, a lucrative business contract by pleasing a client, and so on. All these initial successes are like the student getting a good grade by pleasing the teacher. Whether you are successful in your new job once you have it, whether you are successful as an actor, grocer, teacher, or whatever, will ultimately depend on how you connect to whatever activity your job requires.

What does it mean to connect directly to an activity? First, consider professional success. The purpose of all professions is to make a product. For instance, doctors cultivate health, architects design buildings, playwrights write plays, and so on. Many people view their work-related activities merely as instruments for producing products. They don't value the process that leads to the product as an end in itself. The ones who do, however, are the ones who become most successful. The student who loves to study, the boxer who loves to box, the runner who loves to run, the farmer who loves to farm all experience the same joy of activity. They love the *process*, not just the product, and so they succeed to a much greater degree.

Suppose you repair bicycles. Fixing bicycles is the process. A fixed bicycle is the product. You want to be a successful bicycle repairer. How? You can't be successful unless you please your clients. You must turn damaged or faulty bicycles into good ones, and you must do it efficiently and well. You can do this at a minimal level if you merely want to please your customers. You can do it much better if you love to repair bicycles.

But every activity, every process, it would seem, has its drudgery. In bicycle repair, you have to repack the ball bearings, grease the chains, adjust the cables. Ordinarily, such chores are drudgery because, as we do them, we focus on getting them done instead of on doing them. When we focus on getting them done we are not all there. Our hands are there and perhaps part of our minds are there, but another part of us constantly projects into the future. If we are completely there, focused on our activity, paying attention to everything we do, our activity, no matter what it is, will rarely be drudgery. Almost always, our desire to get it over with makes it drudgery.

Suppose, for instance, you are told to set up and then dismantle a toy city. It will take hours of patient, detailed work to set up the city, which will only be destroyed in the end. How would you react? As you were doing it, you'd probably be thinking, What is the purpose of this? I want to finish, get some sleep before I have to go to work, and so on.

Yet when we were children, we played like that for hours on end. Did we worry then about the purpose of building toy cities that would be dismantled as soon as we finished? What was the purpose of building them? Wasn't it simply the act of doing it? When we were children, we played games not to be done with them but to do them. That's why we enjoyed them so much. Isn't that the source of the magic of childhood?

Living is a series of activities that involves everything you do, including your job. Living is your activity. The product is *you*. Being connected to your life means, ultimately, being connected to all the activities of your life. These activities continually produce new versions of you. Being connected means valuing these activities not merely as a means to an end—as a means to producing a certain type of you—but rather as ends in themselves.

Consider, for example, the activity of keeping yourself physically fit. It can be done primarily as an end in itself. Or it can be done as a mere means to fitness. Ask yourself this: Who will be more physically fit after five years—the person who flogs himself into jogging every morning or the person who so enjoys the physical act of running that she does it willingly every day?

If in all your activities the thing you focus on is the finished product—the read book, the fixed bicycle, the delivered mail, the college degree, the ideal you—happiness might surface briefly after you have completed something, but then it is usually time to start something else. Then you rush through the next project, struggling with yourself because you don't really want to be doing it either. You just want to have done it, to be finished.

If you are connected to the process, the main reward isn't with the finishing. It's with the doing. The finishing may even have a sorrowful aspect because it will signify the end of a particular process. For the authors of this book, for instance, when the last word is written, when the final revision is sent off to the publisher, there will be joy. There will also be sorrow because a process they love will have ended. There might be other books, other processes. But *this* particular process will have ended forever.

So also with the process of being a person. When a life that has been good is nearing completion, there will be sorrow. There might also be the joy of completion. There might even be other lives. But *this* life, *this* particular process, will have ended forever.

The key to success in life, then, is connecting not with a product but with a process: ultimately, with the process of being yourself. Where there is genuine connection to a process, there will be success. Success makes our lives rich and full of meaning. And where there is success, ultimately there will also be sorrow because it is the nature of all processes to change, and by changing they end.

What, then, about the meaning of life?

The many answers that have been given, as we have suggested, are answers to the wrong question. They attempt to tell us the meaning of life when what we need is a solution to life's struggles. The real question is "Why is life such a struggle?"

You now have an answer: Life is a struggle because you are divided against others and also against yourself. But do you now have a solution to life's struggles? No. You remain divided. You remain struggling. Why?

Looking for answers is looking in the wrong place. Answers are not the answer. What you need is what none who live attached to answers have: the wisdom to live without being divided and to connect directly to the *process* that is your life.

ETHICS

From childhood on you are told not just who you are and what the world is, but what to do and how to do it, what to think and how to think it, how to talk and whom to talk to, what to say and when to say it, what not to say and when not to say it, whom to listen to and whom not to, what matters most and what matters least, what's proper and what isn't, what's right and what's wrong, which goals to seek and which not to, when to have sex and when not to, and with whom, and why; good words, bad words, good music, bad music, good books, bad books, good people, bad people; how to dress, how to walk, how to eat, whom to trust, how to behave, how to treat others, how to treat yourself, how to become secure, rich, successful, happy—the list is endless. The advice is endless. And it will continue until you die.

Parents, teachers, lawmakers, politicians, and religious leaders are trying to train you how to fit into the world they inherited from their parents, teachers, lawmakers, politicians, and religious leaders, who in turn inherited it from their authorities, and so on. Why are they doing this?

Obvious answer: You need to be trained to behave well, think well, live well, and so on, because you are by nature bad. Left to your own devices, you would think the wrong thoughts, say the wrong things, feel the wrong emotions, and behave terribly toward others. Without proper training you would lead yourself and others to ruin. You need social, political, and religious leaders to keep you in line.

All of us, especially when we are very young, need the help of parents and others both to nurture us and to keep us from hurting ourselves. Infants need everything provided for them. And even young children need constant supervision and occasional guidance for their own good. But surely the amount of training to which each of us is subjected goes way beyond what we need to keep from hurting ourselves. What's happening is that people are molding us in accordance with their conception of what it is to be a good person. Left to our own devices, apparently, we would surely become bad people. It is as if by nature we are bad and only by their training can we become good.

But first, how do the authorities in charge of your conditioning know you are by nature bad? Without authorities constantly trying to condition you—trying to get you to believe and behave as they want you to believe and behave—you *might* grow up at least as good as you are now. Perhaps authorities know through experience that all people are by nature bad. But how could they know this through experience? When were people ever allowed to discover for themselves, without being prodded by some authority or other, what life is all about and to decide for themselves how best to live?

There has never been a time, in recorded history, when people have not been conditioned by social, political, or religious leaders. So the assumption that without being trained by authorities you would be bad has never been tested. Rather, the assumption has simply been passed down, generation after generation, from one authority to another, without question, perhaps because authorities find it convenient not to question the assumption that they, the authorities, are indispensable—that without them to keep us in line we would all run amok.

Second, if all people are naturally bad, won't the people who become authorities also be bad? The only difference will be that besides being bad, the authorities will be powerful. Unless in the process of being trained or of gaining power over others bad people are reliably transformed into good people, the tradition of authority will generally give rise to a world in which a bunch of bad, powerful people have dominion over a bunch of bad, weak people. Becoming an authority might even make a person worse: "Power corrupts, and absolute power corrupts absolutely."

Third, why do the leaders who have so many answers have so many problems? The same people who are training you how to think and act and feel are trying (so they say) to spare you from problems that (and this they conveniently fail to mention) they have not managed to avoid themselves. Their thoughts are often confused, their actions callous and reprehensible, their lives a painful struggle. If the trainers are giving you what their trainers gave them, then perhaps not only is the training not working, the training may well be the source of the problem.

Fourth, and most importantly, how do social, political, and religious authorities know what's best? Perhaps it's simply a case of "Father knows best." Since the beginning of recorded history, the people in charge have nearly always been males. Males as heads of families, males as heads of state, males as the great philosophers, males as the great writers, males as the great painters, musicians, and inventors, males as originators of religion, and, finally, males as God. Perhaps the problem is that the trainers in charge of the training have been males!

That males have been the problem is probably as close to absolute truth as one can get in a relativistic universe. However, when women become leaders they can be as insufferable, dogmatic, power-hungry, corrupt, and vicious as the worst of males. Of course, women have had to wrestle power away from men within an already patriarchal society. Perhaps in a society created and controlled by women, women would be better trainers than men have ever been. But the question is not whether women would be better trainers than men. The question is whether we need trainers at all. "Mother knows best" is just a variation of "Father knows best." What reason is there for thinking that *anybody* knows best?

One would certainly think that so many authorities with so many answers would have succeeded in creating societies in which people live wonderful, happy, successful lives. But their track record doesn't exactly take one's breath away (except, perhaps, literally). Maybe there is no alternative to authority and we are stuck. But if whipping a horse won't make it go faster, why beat the poor beast?

Perhaps the authorities know that, in the long run, the method of authority will get you to where you ought to be. But how do they know that? Traditionally, the answer—the grand bulwark of authority—has been "God." *He* passes down truths about how you should live. Your job is to learn God's truths and that takes training. Invariably, however, for some reason God chooses to pass these truths down not to *you* but to *them,* usually to whoever is already in power. Why God would choose to reveal the truth only to some religious and political middle*men* instead of to everybody is perhaps one of those mysterious, wondrous ways God works.

But even if God does hand down to a few choice authorities truths about how you should live, how do you know which authorities are the genuine ones? God doesn't extend a hand from the sky and point them out to you. It is conveniently left to the authorities themselves to enlighten you about who the proper authorities are.

Invariably, they point to themselves or to members of their own groups, disagreeing vehemently among themselves about who the proper authorities are—often to the point of killing each other or (more usually) inspiring their followers to do the killing and dying.

So, how do you know which "divinely inspired" truths are the real ones? You could just pick whichever ones your own authorities have taught you and leave it at that. But that would be arbitrary. And, anyway, *why* should you do this? Because your authorities say so? Why should you listen? Because that's what they say is best for you? How do they *know* what is best for you? Because God told them? How do *you* know God told them? Because *they* say so? How do you know the authorities aren't lying or deceived? You don't. So even if some authorities do get their truths from God, it doesn't do you any good. And simply supposing that they do has led, historically, to intolerance, violence, bloodshed, suffering, repression, confusion, fear, hatred, and death.

Perhaps, though, some authorities get their truths not from God but from reason. If that were the case, that might work for them, but what about you? The first problem, once again, is that even the authorities who claim to rely on reason disagree about what reason dictates. How do you know which secular authorities to trust? If comparably credentialed authorities disagree, then those who are not authorities have no basis for believing one authority rather than another.

In addition, just as you have ample reason to suspect that religious authorities are not genuine authorities on how you should live, so you have ample reason to suspect that secular authorities are not genuine authorities on how you should live. Their performance thus far is hardly inspiring. For instance, secular believers in the power of reason have pleaded and plotted for centuries for a chance to seize the reins of political power from believers in God. Finally, in the twentieth century, they got their chance. Some improvement! Secular political authorities who claim their answers are based not on faith but on reason have been just as ruthless, dogmatic, corrupt, and vicious as their religious counterparts. If secular leaders have succeeded in showing that the authority of reason is greater than the authority of faith, they have also showed that the problem is not with the basis of authority but that authority may well be the basis of the problem.

One problem is that authorities tend to want to preserve their positions of authority, regardless of whether they are in the right or in the wrong, by establishing a set of societal and legal procedures that not only preserve their power but increase it over time. By creating a social structure in which their threats can be carried out, they can make it true that accepting what they *claim* is best for you *is* best for you. If you don't obey, you'll get hurt—*by them!* They can say, as fathers often do, "You'd better listen if you know what's good for you"—not as a way of showing rationally that what they claim is in your best interest really is in your best interest, but as a way of using their position of power to subjugate your will to theirs. But unless the authorities know that whatever you are being ordered to do really is in your best interest (Is it? How do they know?), and unless you know that the authorities have your interests in mind (Do they? How do you know?) rather than their own, obedience to authority does not solve the problem of how best to live. And unless the authorities are on the right track, obedience may lead you further astray and possibly destroy you.

What, then, ought you to do? Perhaps you should ignore external authorities and rely instead on the internal authority of your own conscience to tell you what is right and what is wrong, how to behave, what your values should be, and so on.

However, most of the same problems that arose in the case of external authority arise also for conscience. Just as the external authorities disagree, so do the dictates of conscience. Different people have radically different intuitions, feelings, attitudes, and so on about how best to live. Why should you trust even the internal authority of your own conscience?

Our consciences seem to vary too much with culture and conditioning to be doorways to the truth. For instance, most Americans who would be repulsed by the sight of someone cooking and eating a dog have no trouble eating cows. Yet most (Asian) Indians would be more horrified by the sight of someone killing and eating a cow than of someone killing and eating a dog. Such sympathies arise as a result of conditioning by various social, religious, and political authorities. Or, to take another example, a white American male of the early nineteenth century would probably be repulsed by the sight of a black man and a white woman kissing. Even today, interracial love affairs give many people bad feelings. Such feelings are merely the result of antiquated traditions, which in turn are the result of conditioning, which in turn is the result of social, religious, and political authorities at work telling you what to think, what to feel, and how to behave, all for your own good. Which leads straight to the possibility that conscience is but external authority internalized.

Familial, societal, religious, and political ideologies have been so ingrained in most of us that they speak to us from within, guiding us with our own feelings. But why then trust your feelings? If morality cannot be based on authority, and if conscience is merely the result of deeply ingrained conditioning—merely external authority internalized—then morality cannot be based on conscience. What reason, then, is there to trust *anybody* for moral guidance—*including yourself?*

But if there is nothing and nobody you can trust for moral guidance, where does that leave you?

VALUES

14

All your life you've been told to adopt ideals, to see yourself—your family, your nationality, your race, your culture, your world—through the tinted lenses of inherited values. You've been taught to label everything yes or no, good or bad, right or wrong, and to appeal to authorities and, through them, to stick ready-made answers onto everything.

Most people fall into line. Those few who rebel and march to the beat of a different drummer usually still march, following, in their rebellion, a path paved with values not of their own but of their peers. Even those who resolve to follow only their own personal consciences follow a conscience that is itself largely the product of elaborate social and cultural conditioning.

Meanwhile, almost everyone is obsessed with two practical questions: What do I want? and How can I get it? Ironically (but not surprisingly, given the external sources of most of our values), when we get what we want, often we no longer want it (and then we can't get rid of it!). Or if we do still want it, either we can't keep it or else it is not enough; we want more. And if and when we get more, that too is ultimately not satisfying. The result, often, is a frustration that breeds deep cynicism, consoled, if at all, only by the grim realization that it may not matter all that much in the end anyway because (so far as we know) what awaits us in the end is just death and then worms.

Everything and everybody now alive will someday be dead; humanity itself will become extinct; the sun will blow up; the books will burn; the statues will melt; the cities will be annihilated. There will be nothing left, not even Earth; the whole universe will ultimately implode itself out of existence or die a slow heat-death.

If nothingness or ashes is the destiny of everything, what it all comes to in the end, what, then, is the value *of* our lives? What should be the values *in* our lives? Is there something meaningful and valuable we can do, or are we just cows stuck on a conveyor belt on the way to the saw?

We can't, it seems, avoid the saw; we can't last forever. Nor can any of the things we create last forever. We can, however, be here fully for the time we do have by making our lives our own. Otherwise, it is as if we never even existed except as placeholders, receptacles for conditioning, or—if we become authorities—conveyor belts for transmitting unexamined answers, like cultural debris, from our conditioners to those we ourselves condition.

By examining our lives, we may be able to wrest ourselves from inherited answers and hand-me-down values long enough to make contact—not with pipe dreams or idealizations—but with what is true and authentic about ourselves and the world. While we may not, ultimately, save ourselves, we can stand up to the disintegrating universe, our destroyer, and in the midst of our annihilation take stock of what is really going on before the world hurtles us and then itself into oblivion. But how?

By the time the idea of questioning your values even occurs to you, you have already internalized so many values that if you try to question these values while remaining committed to them, your questioning is likely to be inauthentic or, at the very least, limited and limiting. It would entail accepting without question many of the very value-assumptions you were trying to question. Perhaps this is the best we can do. But it would be revealing if we could get entirely outside our frameworks of values, beyond their scope, to get a neutral perspective on them (if there even is such a thing as a neutral perspective).

To do so, we would have to let go of our values long enough for them to let go of us. The Christian would have to cease being a Christian, the American would have to cease being an American, the Communist would have to cease being a Communist, and so on— not in the sense of ceasing to be affiliated with whatever religious, national, or political group generates whatever set of values one subscribes to—but in the sense of suspending commitment to these values. We would have to set aside our familial and cultural values and get beyond even our consciences—not necessarily for the purpose of dispensing permanently with these values or to attach ourselves to some new values, but as an exercise in getting temporarily far enough beyond the scope of our values so that we can at least examine them without presupposing the very values we are examining, or any other values, except for the value of seeing ourselves and the world exactly as we are.

The question, then, is how to unhook your thoughts and feelings from whatever value-anchors now secure and bind you to your present point of view. It's unrealistic to suppose you can simply drop all your values—that is, that you can just stop expressing any of your values to others and even stop thinking them (consciously or unconsciously) to yourself. Your values—your ideas about right and wrong, good and bad, beautiful and ugly, and so on—are so inextricably bound up with your inner and outer life (for instance, with the structure of your motivations as well as with which actions you perform) that there is no practical way to just delete your values, without putting anything in their place, and still live a recognizably human life.

However, it may be possible to develop the practice of substituting for those value judgments you express in your speech and thought the factual judgments you would use to justify your value judgments if you were asked to do so. So, for instance, instead of saying (or thinking) that abortion is *morally wrong* (a value judgment), you could say that abortion generally results in the destruction of a fetus that hasn't yet intentionally done anything to cause pain and that has the potential to become a normal, conscious adult human being (a factual judgment), and that women often are traumatized by allowing their fetuses to be killed (a factual judgment). Or instead of saying that abortion is *morally permissible* (a value judgment), you could say that a fetus is not a conscious being (a factual judgment) and that, generally, women are more traumatized by giving birth to unwanted children than by aborting unwanted fetuses (a factual judgment). (Note that calling a judgment *factual* does not by itself imply that the judgment is correct but merely that it is a judgment about *facts*. Thus some factual judgments are true, some false, depending on what the *actual* facts are.)

Similarly, instead of saying (or thinking) that it is *good* to be sincere in talking with other people (a value judgment), you could say that being sincere usually promotes mutual understanding and trust (a factual judgment). Instead of saying (or thinking) that Siesta Key is a *more beautiful* beach in Florida than Fort Lauderdale (a value judgment), you could say that Siesta Key is a wider beach and has whiter, cleaner sand (a factual judgment).

The crucial distinction for this exercise in substitution is that between values and facts. While it may be a difficult distinction, its basic contours can be illustrated in terms of simple examples. The judgment, for instance, that Siesta Key is *more beautiful* than Fort Lauderdale is a value judgment in that it expresses a pro (or con) attitude and in that there is no reason to think that the relationship "more beautiful than" exists independently of such attitudes. The judgment that Siesta Key is a *wider* beach than Fort Lauderdale, on the other hand, is a factual judgment in that it describes a certain relationship that exists in the world without expressing a pro or con attitude toward that relationship.

It is essential to the meaning of a value judgment—but not to the meaning of a factual judgment—that it expresses a pro or con attitude. The preceding examples showed a con or pro attitude toward abortion, a pro attitude toward sincerity, and a pro attitude toward Siesta Key beach as compared to Fort Lauderdale beach.

In addition, accepted techniques can determine whether most factual judgments are true. To determine whether Siesta Key is a wider beach than Fort Lauderdale, we can measure them. Sometimes accepted techniques can also determine whether value judgments are true. Thus we have accepted techniques for determining whether a strawberry is red and sweet, and a red, sweet strawberry will almost invariably taste *better* than a green, sour one. However, whereas determining the truth of factual judgments involves showing that other *factual* judgments are true, determining the truth of value judgments, if we can determine their truth at all, rarely, if ever, involves showing just that other *value* judgments are true. Rather, as in the strawberry example, it involves showing that other *factual* judgments are true. It seems, then, that factual judgments are more fundamental than value judgments in that value judgments depend on factual judgments but not vice versa.

It is often more convenient to use a value judgment than to report the factual evidence that we would give to justify it. But convenience aside, it is nearly always possible for us to replace a value judgment with our factual evidence for it. In other words, even though value judgments and factual judgments may mean different things, if the only reasons we would give to support a value judgment are factual judgments, then most of the time we could just report our factual evidence and thereby avoid the value judgment.

There are two possible problems with this strategy of substituting factual judgments for value judgments. First, the demarcation between values and facts is often fuzzy. The judgment that dinner was delicious, for instance, is not easily classified as either evaluative or factual. Second, if we continue the analysis of our techniques for determining the truth of factual judgments far enough, perhaps all the way to the end (if there is an end), value judgments may reemerge. For instance, our views about whether God exists (a factual matter) may, in the final analysis, be influenced by our commitment to the rule that, all else being equal, simpler explanations are more worthy of belief than complex ones. And our commitment to this (or some such) rule, may, again in the final analysis, be an expression of our values.

Such complications suggest that it is difficult to draw a sharp distinction between values and facts. However, they do not show that the option of dropping the values we express in our thoughts and judgments—at least temporarily, for the purpose of examining them—is unrealistic. Although the demarcation between values and facts may be fuzzy, and we may not be able to define the difference precisely, we can distinguish clear cases of values from clear cases of facts. An ability to distinguish clear cases must be more basic than the ability to define the distinction between value and fact because to define this distinction we would first have to recognize clear cases of both values and facts; otherwise we wouldn't be able to understand the distinction our definition was designed to capture.

The ability to distinguish clear cases of values from clear cases of facts is all you need, theoretically, to replace your value judgments with factual judgments. Even if many cases are borderline, and even if some procedural values still lurk far in the background, you could step out of almost all of your inherited frameworks of values if you could drop all clear cases of value judgments and replace them with the underlying factual judgments you would ordinarily give to justify them. That is, if you could stop not only expressing your values to others but also thinking them privately to yourself, you could then examine and critically assess your previous involvement with your values, not through the tinted lenses that these values themselves provide, but from a vantage point beyond their scope.

Will the strategy of replacing value judgments with the underlying factual evidence on which they are based work across the board, or are there some cases where you cannot make the replacement because you have no underlying reasons for your value judgments? For instance, suppose you think some painting is beautiful—not because of its colors, shapes, textures, and the relationships among its visual elements—that is, not because of anything about the way the painting looks—but "just because." Your evaluation of the painting, in this case, is arbitrary in that it is independent of the painting's properties as well as independent of any further value considerations. If the only reason for saying that evaluations are not expendable is that we need them to make arbitrary evaluative judgments, then the question is whether we can get along as well or better without making arbitrary evaluative judgments. It seems we can.

A second possibility is that you have factual evidence for your value judgment that the painting is beautiful (so your judgment is not arbitrary), but you can't say what your evidence is and so you can't substitute your factual evidence for your value judgment. In this case, since your value judgment is not arbitrary, you would lose something if you jettisoned it without replacing it. And since you can't say what the factual evidence is upon which your value judgments are based (even though we are now supposing you have such evidence), you can't replace your judgment with a report of this evidence.

But in that case, your inability to report the factual evidence underlying your value judgment must be either because you don't know what that evidence is or because you know what it is but can't put it into words. If you don't know what the facts underlying your value judgment are, then how do you know that there are any facts underlying your value judgment? If your assumption that your evaluation is grounded in facts is itself (so far as you know) arbitrary, then so is your value judgment. If, on the other hand, you have factual evidence *that you have factual evidence*, then you can report that *secondary* factual evidence instead of the value judgment.

Suppose, for instance, that you have factual evidence and you know that you have such evidence (perhaps by knowing what it is), but you can't put your evidence into words. Then you could at least put *that* into words. Instead of saying that you like the painting because it is beautiful, you could say that you like it for reasons you can't put into words. It's not clear that the first way of expressing yourself—evaluatively—is any better than the second way of expressing yourself—factually. Hence, it's hard to see what you would lose by dropping the evaluation.

A final possibility is that you have evidence for your value judgment (so it is not arbitrary), but your evidence is not factual evidence. What, then, could your evidence be? The only thing it seems it could be is simply your perception that the painting is beautiful, not because of any of its factual properties, but just beautiful per se.

The question, then, would be how you get access to this mysterious "evidence" that is not factual evidence. Our ordinary sense organs are capable of responding just to factual stimulation—sound waves, light waves, pressure, and so on. If you have access to evidence that is not ultimately physical stimulation, then it must be because you have a special organ for acquiring such evidence. Some people have actually thought that we do have "evaluative organs" (and some, perhaps, still think this); for instance, some eighteenth-century ethicists used to think that, in addition to the senses we share with the higher animals, humans have a "moral sense." But no one has ever been able to locate this phantom organ or explain how it works to pick up evaluative information from the world. Today few people are persuaded by such theories.

If you always give the factual reasons for your value judgments instead of making the value judgments themselves, *you* will stick to the facts. Other people, if they wanted to, could draw their own evaluative conclusions. However, the people to whom you would communicate factually would not *have* to draw their own evaluative conclusions. They could, if they wanted to, stick to the facts and respond accordingly. For instance, if instead of telling people that you are good at chess, you told them that you are a grand master, then they, instead of concluding that you are good at chess, could turn down your offer to play for money. Their reason would not have to be (the evaluative one) that you are better than they are, but rather (the factual one) that if they play against you, they will probably lose. Thus the policy of substituting factual judgments for value judgments is not necessarily just a way of shuffling value judgments around—moving them, say, from your mouth to other mouths—but potentially of eliminating altogether those value judgments we express to one another.

Even so, you might well have grave doubts about whether this program of substituting factual judgments for value judgments is realistic. Perhaps, with practice, you could stop expressing your values to others. But could you also stop thinking value judgments privately to yourself? And even if you could, wouldn't the practice of doing so impoverish your life?

The question now is not just one of communication. You could stop making value judgments to others simply by being quiet. To stop making them to yourself, you would have to stop *thinking* them—you would have to drop all your evaluative beliefs. If the earlier policy of not communicating your values to others would be a significant step, this new policy of not even thinking them would be a monumental leap.

Making a value judgment to yourself is a form of communicating to yourself. (As someone once remarked, "How do I know what I'm thinking until I hear what I'm saying?") To communicate with others you have to form the judgment and also express it publicly, whereas to communicate with yourself you have only to form the judgment—to think it. Still, if you could live your life without communicating your values to others, couldn't you live your life—perhaps as easily—without communicating them to yourself?

Surprisingly, you could live your life almost as easily and in exactly the same way. However difficult it might be in practice to break the habit of making value judgments, in theory you could refrain from making them. Either you could be (internally) silent or you could think only about the relevant underlying facts. It would be difficult because our evaluative habits are so deeply ingrained and because speech is more easily controlled than thought. But because external silence or the substitution of factual judgments for overt value judgments is possible, internal silence or a similar internal substitution must also be possible, and for exactly the same reasons. Thus you could eliminate all clear cases of value judgments—without qualification (except perhaps for the procedural value judgments mentioned earlier that may underlie our methods for determining facts).

It is sometimes said that a life without values would be impossible or at least not recognizably human. Interestingly, though, if you could refrain from making or thinking any value judgments, others could as well. In theory, then, we could see ourselves and the world without values—seemingly without losing anything that is essential to our lives.

The elimination of all value judgments (including those that are merely thought) is tantamount to the elimination of values. For where do values exist except in our minds? Thus we could, in theory, take the truly radical step of actually creating a recognizably human world without any values whatsoever—not just a world without objective values (we may already have that) but a world without even subjective values.

In a world without values we would have to stop judging ourselves and each other evaluatively. When you judge yourself evaluatively, you compare yourself either to yourself at a different time, or to someone else, or to some idealized person—perhaps the "you" that you, your family, or your friends would like you to be. Because most of us spend a lot of time and energy in the often unpleasant task of comparing ourselves evaluatively, our lives would be quite different if we stopped. No one likes to be constantly judged, and self-judgment can be more oppressive than external evaluation; so it seems that to this extent, at least, our lives might be less oppressive and happier if we gave up comparing ourselves evaluatively.

Even if we were to give up judging ourselves evaluatively, we could still make factual comparisons, even ones right on the threshold of being evaluative. For instance, the judgment that you got an A in every course you took last semester (whether or not it is true) is a factual judgment. So is the judgment that someone else thinks you are a good student. For that matter, so is the judgment that you once thought you were a good student, if you are simply reporting what you once thought and not endorsing the thought. On the other hand, the endorsed judgment that you actually are a good student is evaluative.

In sum, if you gave up comparing yourself and others evaluatively, you could still make factual comparisons. The only difference (perhaps an important one) is that you would not express any pro or con attitude on the value of these comparisons. For instance, you could note that your cumulative grade average in college is B+, as compared to the collegewide average of C+, but you could not even *think* that it is *better* to have a higher than a lower grade average. You could, of course, recognize that graduates with higher averages tend to get higher-paying jobs, but you could not even think that it is good to get a higher-paying job.

It may seem, then, that dropping all evaluative comparisons would radically undercut your motivation. If you didn't think that getting a B+ is better than getting a B–, what possible motive could you have to do the extra work to get a B+? Surprisingly, your motives would probably remain about the same. For instance, you might do the extra work because you want a higher-salaried job after you graduate. But why want a higher-salaried job if it isn't *better* than a lower-salaried job? Again, for your same old reasons: say, because then you will have enough money to buy new clothes and pay the rent for the house you prefer to live in. But why want those things if they are not *better?* Ultimately because you think they will please you.

Isn't it better to be pleased than not? Perhaps. But the mere fact that something pleases you (a factual matter) may be motive enough for doing it. The value judgment that it is better to do things that please you is motivationally redundant. There is, then, no reason to think that dropping all value judgments would undercut your motivation to pursue your goals. You would be deprived of evaluative reasons for being motivated, but to the extent that you rely on such reasons, they could easily be replaced by factual reasons. In sum, as far as motivation is concerned, nothing would be lost.

Would anything be added by seeing yourself without values? Two things: clarity and immediacy. Dropping evaluative judgments and replacing them with the factual judgments on which they are based would force you to get clearer about why you have the preferences and aversions you do. The evaluative judgment "Because it's good (or bad)" as a response to the question of why you like (or dislike) something is about as informative as saying "Just because." The factual basis for your evaluation will almost always be more informative.

With evaluations available, often we don't go to the trouble of getting clear about what lies behind them. We're lazy, and it's easier to give our evaluative summation and leave the factual underpinnings implicit and murky. This makes evaluation dangerous as a self-deceptive tool. For instance, someone who is suffering from extreme guilt can say "I'm bad" rather than focusing on the underlying cause of the guilt, such as parental disapproval. Or a student doing poorly in a class can say "I'm a bad student" rather than focusing on the facts underlying the problem, such as ineffective study habits. Negative evaluations thus often get locked into our psyches and block access to the neutral factual information that provoked them in the first place. That's why in psychotherapy, for instance, a person who thinks he is "bad" can contribute importantly to his cure simply by telling the therapist (and himself) exactly (and neutrally) what lies behind his self-condemnation.

Factual judgments are more immediate than value judgments because they are more fundamental. The evaluative judgment that something is "good" is often little more than an objectified version of the more personal judgment that you liked it. The more immediate fact is that you liked it. The judgment that it is good is evaluative packaging. Just as people in positions of authority often wear uniforms to impress us, it is as if we dress up our naked personal preferences in objective trappings before sending them out into the world.

The depersonalized and objectifying features of value judgments are a distancing mechanism—a way of going beyond and away from our personal reactions. In distancing ourselves from our personal preferences through evaluative language, we camouflage the fact that we are claiming more than mere personal preference would warrant. The evaluative move thus not only adds a theoretical layer to how we conceptualize the psychological reality of our lives but also portrays our personal preferences as if they were something more and grander than they are.

Unclothed of your values, you would stand naked, no longer judging your life evaluatively but simply living it; no longer judging the lives of others evaluatively but simply interacting with them. It seems, then, that replacing your value judgments with the factual evidence that supports them is not only theoretically possible but is a way of stepping outside your value frameworks and seeing yourself and your values more neutrally.

There is a second way of getting outside the framework of your values. This way does not require that you stop making value judgments but only that you (nonevaluatively) watch yourself making them. That is, you try to understand the role of your values in your life, not by taking anything away from your thought or behavior (such as your value judgments) but by adding something to them— a nonjudging awareness of exactly what you are doing and why you are doing it—so that you can understand experientially what your values are and how they affect your life and the lives of others.

Most of us can separate (dissociate) a part of our subjective lives from the rest of ourselves. The part you would dissociate, then, becomes a neutral watcher of the rest of your experience and behavior, including your judging behavior. That is, with the part of your awareness that is dissociated from the rest, you look at everything in which you are involved without saying yes or no to anything that happens, to what you do, to what happens to you, to your experiences, to what other people do, and so on. Your pleasures, pains, sensations, thoughts, and emotions are allowed to continue without this dissociated part of yourself—the "watcher"—trying to direct the show. The watcher is simply there with your life, aware of what is happening but not judging it, perhaps more aware of yourself than you ordinarily are, even than you've ever been, because now your values are out of the way. Yet the watcher is just a neutral observer, not trying to make anything happen, not trying to stop anything from happening, just watching. Even when this neutral part of you is aware that another part of you is involved in evaluative judgments, the neutral part does not need to participate in those judgments; rather, it can just watch the judging without either identifying with it or judging it. For instance, if this neutral part of you is aware that another part of you is proud (a judgmental reaction), it does not have to identify with the pride or judge it; it can just watch.

The question, then, is whether you can locate within yourself a neutral center of awareness that is beyond all your theories and answers about good and bad, right and wrong, beautiful and ugly, and so on. And can you be neutral with yourself for long enough that your values and judgments seem like the values and judgments of someone else—items in the world that arouse your interest and for which you are aware of how they affect the bodies and minds you are watching? In other words, can you dissociate a part of yourself that is just a presence, aware of everything going on at the moment but not identified with anything, beyond values and theories and attitudes and answers? Can you be consumed by the utterly simple, unuttered question "What is this?" And at the next moment: "And what is this?" "And this?" "And this?"—never gathering it all up, never theorizing, just watching every experience, emotion, thought, and movement? In short, can you watch your values without identifying with them, without the neutral watcher within you owning them as *its* values?

This may seem a strange and artificial exercise, but it can be revealing. If the values you are watching are not really "your" values—not the values of the watcher, anyway—inevitably the question arises: If I am the watcher, who, then, is the other? Who is the one being watched, the conditioned one, the posturing one, the one with the answers, the views, with the yes's and no's, this strange alien person that from this neutral perspective hardly even seems a person but, rather, more like an organism, a biological and psychological mechanism programmed by its culture like some kind of elaborate wind-up toy, different now from you-the-watcher? If without thinking or theorizing, without gathering up the insights, you can just watch each moment come and go, letting that awareness in you be distanced from what is being watched, freed of that body–mind complex, then later when you return to the values that before were so familiar, so close to you they stuck like glue, they are now all strangeness.

What is your life from this neutral vantage point that is not even really a vantage point on a life that is not even "your" life? What can you learn? Perhaps that "you," the watcher, do not feel like the same person as this mind–body complex you are watching, that what you are watching is not only a conditioned machine but also an unskillful, clumsy machine (not that you judge this; rather, you just see the machine trying for a certain effect as if it—the machine—originated the trying, and then you see it failing by doing something that will never bring about the desired effect but will create exactly the opposite). Perhaps, as you watch, you can see all the genuineness in the situation you are watching leak away, never expressed, never even noticed by the bungling machine lumbering through a life, hurting, often without even noticing that it is hurting. Perhaps you see that what you are watching doesn't mesh well with its environment because it is not just happening but is awkwardly trying for various effects that it unskillfully acts (reacts) to try to bring about, rarely seeing situations clearly for what they are because this thing sees everything only through a cloudy glass of conditioned needs.

If you can observe yourself in this way for a few minutes, even for one minute, even for seven seconds, then for at least that length of time, you are out of the framework of values within which the thing you are watching—what you used to call "yourself"—lives its life. For a time, you—the neutral watcher—are out of it, free from it, but not forever, not even for long, because it sucks you up again as soon as your awareness wavers, like some giant vacuum cleaner that gathers dirt but is unable to clean itself, a valuer, engaged in the world but out of sync, a wobble, every action a reaction, nothing original, nothing new, an echo, distorted, unskillful, full of pain, causing pain, bungling, forever bungling...on the way to the saw.

EPILOGUE

You're standing at the bank of a river, the deepest and most treacherous river on the planet. Yet you want to get to the other side. How will you do it?

You look for a bridge. There are no bridges.

You try to find a boat. There are no boats.

You want to fly across. There are no airplanes.

In frustration, you search for building materials. There are none.

You consider walking around it, but it flows without interruption all the way from the North Pole to the South Pole.

In desperation, you consider swimming. But the river is too wide and too turbulent. Everyone who has ever entered it has drowned. Yet you want to get to the other side. But how?

When others have tried to tunnel under the river, water swelled up through the earth and drowned them. When they tried draining the river, they discovered that its waters are inexhaustible.

You try everything you can think of. Nothing works. The river is uncrossable. Yet you want to get to the other side. How will you do it?

Don't feel bad if you don't know the answer. The question asks what you should do to get to the other side of a river that's uncrossable. Obviously, you can't cross an uncrossable river.

The answer to the question "How do you get to the other side of an uncrossable river?" can't possibly have anything to do with crossing the river. The river is uncrossable. Still, you want to get to the other side. How will you do it?

The question appears unanswerable. If the only purpose in asking questions is to answer them, then it is pointless to try to answer an unanswerable question. But is this the only purpose?

Consider an analogy. Could there be any purpose in having weights that you could not lift? It may seem not. Weights tone up your muscles only if you lift them. Isometrics, however, is a system of exercise in which you tone up your muscles not by lifting weights but by exerting your muscles against each other. For example, you clasp the cupped fingers of your two hands together and strain to pull them apart. In isometrics, it is as if you yourself are the weight, and you are trying to lift yourself. You can't do it—but trying to lift yourself can tone your muscles more efficiently than conventional weight lifting.

Isometrics for your body is like trying to lift unliftable weights. Trying to answer unanswerable questions is like isometrics for your mind. Most philosophy is like isometrics for the mind. Throw your hands up in despair before an unliftable weight and you gain nothing. Throw your hands up in despair before the big, unanswerable questions, and you also gain nothing.

Notice, too, how most of us have been conditioned *not* to ask unanswerable questions. We have been conditioned to assume that there is no point to it. We never consider the possibility that one purpose of asking unanswerable questions might be to tone up your mental muscles. What is more surprising is that there is yet another, even more important, purpose to asking, and to keep on asking, unanswerable questions.

You're standing on the bank of the river. You want to get to the other side. How will you do it? You've exhausted all the traditional answers. What's left? Nontraditional answers. When we are desperate for a solution but the traditional answers don't work, we must try nontraditional answers. And to find nontraditional answers to seemingly unanswerable questions, we must drop some of our assumptions about the question and the limits within which it can be answered. Thus trying to answer seemingly unanswerable questions not only strengthens the mind but also expands it.

Consider the following seemingly unanswerable question: "What is the shortest distance between two points that is even shorter than a straight line?" If you're mathematically sophisticated you know this is unanswerable only within the framework of traditional, Euclidean geometry. If you drop one of the old assumptions about parallel lines—the postulate that two parallel lines can never meet—the question can then be answered within the framework of a non-Euclidean geometry. The answer is "A curved line."

In other words, questions are neither answerable nor unanswerable *without qualification*. There are no *absolutely* unanswerable questions—absolutely none! There are only *conditionally* unanswerable

questions. And there are no *absolutely* answerable questions—
absolutely none. There are only *conditionally* answerable questions.
Whether a question is answerable or unanswerable depends on the
assumptions of the person trying to answer it.

Given the assumptions of Euclidean geometry, the question
"What is the shortest distance between two points that is even
shorter than a straight line?" is unanswerable. Given the different assumptions of the non-Euclidean geometry of curved spaces, the
question *has* an answer.

So how do you get to the other side of an uncrossable river?
How do we find answers to questions that, as far as we know, are
unanswerable?

We do it by dropping some assumptions. But which? If the river
is uncrossable, which assumption could we drop that would get us
to the other side? There seems to be just one: the assumption that if
you're on one side of a river, you're not already on the other side.

It might seem crazy to drop this assumption, but it's crazy only
if we can't imagine how the assumption could be false. We can. Picture the river from space: You see a line extending from the northern
tip to the southern tip of a spherical planet. This line is uncrossable.
Imagine a point on one side of the line. How could this point get to
the other side of the uncrossable line?

It's easy. Imagine that the point faces away from the line and
starts walking. Since it never crosses the line and the side of the river
it's on extends all the way around the globe, it never leaves its side,
yet it gets to the other side. The point doesn't even have to do any
walking to get to the other side. Walking didn't get it to the other
side. Walking just made it obvious that the point was already on the
other side.

The uncrossable line has only one side. The uncrossable river
also has only one side. So how do you get to the other side of the uncrossable river?

It's easy. You don't have to do anything. You're already there.

PHILOSOPHICAL CONNECTIONS

CHAPTER 1 **WHERE**

'Twill not be surprising after this, if I deliver a maxim,
which is condemn'd by several metaphysicians, and is es-
teem'd contrary to the most certain principles of human
reason. This maxim is *that an object may exist, and yet be no
where:* and I assert, that this is not only possible, but that the
greatest part of beings do and must exist after this manner.

So wrote the great modern philosopher David Hume (in his classic *Treatise
of Human Nature,* 1738), one of the founders of the influential philosophical
movement called British empiricism. These words of his express an idea
that is central to our first chapter. Many students who have read this chapter ask, "Could the universe be in the mind?" There is an important sense
in which it could be (see the readings on idealism for our "Reality" chapter), if one is referring to the universe of our perceptions. Hume argues that
it is "those perceptions which are simple, and exist no where."

For a more sophisticated, contemporary exploration into the concepts
not only of space but also of time, see Hans Reichenbach's *Philosophy of
Space and Time* (Dover, 1958), a modern philosophical classic that takes the
reader on a mind-bending odyssey through the topology of space and time.
For excellent tools to help you visualize some of the strange twists in con-
temporary scientific views of space, see *A Topological Picturebook* by George
K. Francis (Springer, 1987), a delightful, hands-on, how-to book on drawing
mathematical pictures, with lots of mind-bending exercises, and J. R.
Weeks's *The Shape of Space* (Marcel Dekker, 1985). For a thoroughly exciting
visual experience, see the short mathematical animation video *Not Knot* by
David Epstein and Charlie Gunn (put out by the University of Minnesota's
Geometry Center), which introduces the mathematical concepts of knots
and Borromean links, shows how they impose a structure on space, and
takes you inside that structure. For an unusual and offbeat introduction to

non-Euclidean geometry, so relevant to understanding the cosmological concept of space as a whole, try Eugene F. Krause's *Taxicab Geometry: An Adventure in Non-Euclidean Geometry* (Dover, 1986). And for a historical introduction to theories of space and time, see John Losee, *A Historical Introduction to the Philosophy of Science,* 3d ed. (Oxford University Press, 1993).

For an easy and thoroughly exciting account of the concept of infinity, nothing beats Constance Reid's *Introduction to Higher Mathematics for the General Reader* (Thomas Y. Crowell, 1959) except, perhaps, Tobias Danzig's rather more sophisticated but still comprehensible treatise *Number,* 4th ed. (Macmillan, 1967), which Einstein himself called the greatest book about mathematics he had ever read. For a sweeping historical panorama of different models of the cosmos, see Milton Munitz's *Theories of the Universe* (Free Press, 1957).

Daniel C. Dennett's "Where Am I?"—originally published in *Brainstorms* (Bradford Books, 1978) and reprinted in Kolak and Martin, eds., *The Experience of Philosophy,* 5th ed. (Wadsworth, 2002)—brings to light the unobvious mystery of how we locate ourselves. By imagining a situation in which his body is separated from his brain, Dennett shows why even the most obvious apparent fact about you, expressed by your avowal "I am here," is deeply questionable.

In the forty pages of *Cosmic View: The Universe in Forty Jumps* (Day, 1957), Kees Boeke puts the immense scale of the universe into perspective all the way from the galaxies to the center of an atom. In *Powers of Ten* (Freeman, 1982) Philip Morrison takes you on a pictorial tour of the cosmos that starts with two picnickers on a blanket in a park in Chicago, moves all the way up to the swirling galaxies and beyond, and then travels back down to the interior of one of the picnicker's hands, all the way into the heart of an atom.

E. A. Abbott's nineteenth-century classic *Flatland* (Dover, 1952) is probably the most delightful book ever written on space and dimensionality. Abbott's story is a touching fantasy about a square who lives in a two-dimensional world until the day he is whisked into the third dimension. When he returns to Flatland, he has trouble convincing his friends to admit even the possibility that space could have three dimensions. Another superb fantasy is George Gamov's *Mr. Tompkins in Wonderland* (Cambridge University Press, 1940). Written in the style of a third-grade primer, it illustrates without any technical language some of the most startling implications of living in an Einsteinian universe.

CHAPTER 2   **WHEN**

Questions about time—how it "flows," if it even does, whether time is real, the relationships between time and experience, psychological time and

physical time, and so on—are central to the branch of philosophy called
metaphysics. According to the ancient Greek philosophers Parmenides and
Zeno, time and its related concepts, change and motion, are not real but
merely an illusion. A good way to explore Greek philosophy is to read John
Mansley Robinson's *An Introduction to Early Greek Philosophy* (Houghton
Mifflin, 1968). Another ancient Greek, who was one of the great founders
of Western philosophy, Aristotle, tried to counter Zeno's arguments in
his *Physics*, Book IV, with the first relational theory of time. Following Aristotle's thoughts, the great medieval thinker St. Augustine developed a subjective view of time in his classic *Confessions*, Book XI, by arguing that time
is a "protraction" of the mind.

Isaac Newton, the great British physicist, philosopher, and mathematician, developed the famous "absolute" view of time in *Sir Isaac Newton's
Mathematical Principles of Natural Philosophy and His System of the World*, Florian Cajori, ed. (University of California Press, 1962). Newton's views were
rejected by his contemporary, the great German philosopher Gottfried
Leibniz, and were refuted two centuries later by Einstein in his special theory of relativity.

For an introduction to the influential views on time of the twentieth-
century French philosopher Henri Bergson, see his *The Creative Mind: An
Introduction to Metaphysics* (Philosophical Library, 1946); here you will find
an elaboration of the view that the individual moments of our experience
are like imperfect snapshots of the temporal flux of pure duration. Another
early twentieth-century philosopher, John McTaggart, in his *The Nature
of Existence* (Cambridge University Press, 1921–27), advocated temporal
idealism, the view that time is not real and exists only in the mind. For further discussion of the view of time developed in this chapter, see Arthur
Schopenhauer's "The Vanity of Existence" in *The Will to Live*, edited by
Richard Taylor (Frederick Ungar, 1962). For an intriguing exploration of
the relationship among time, thought, and consciousness, see *The Ending of
Time* (Harper & Row, 1985), by experiential philosopher J. Krishnamurti
and theoretical physicist David Bohm.

Wesley C. Salmon's *Space, Time, and Motion: A Philosophical Introduction* (University of Minnesota Press, 1980) is a good place to begin an exploration of Zeno's famous and deeply influential paradoxes; follow this
with Adolph Grunbaum's *Modern Science and Zeno's Paradoxes* (D. Reidel,
1973). To see what happens when a philosopher and a contemporary
mathematician join forces to determine the state of the art of Zeno's paradoxes, see Daniel Kolak and David Goloff, "The Incredible Shrinking
Zeno" (reprinted in Daniel Kolak and Raymond Martin, eds., *The Experience of Philosophy*, 5th ed., Wadsworth, 2002), a refinement of the original

paradox in which they argue that even mathematical solutions, such as summing the infinite series and calculus, fail to solve a perpetually unsolvable paradox that undermines our entire view of reality.

The best popular exposition of Einstein's relativity was written by Einstein himself in his *Relativity* (Crown, 1961). In *The Direction of Time* (University of California Press, 1971), Hans Reichenbach offers a historical survey of the concept of time leading up to the advent of quantum mechanics. For those who want an elementary account, Bertrand Russell's *The ABC of Relativity* (Signet, 1959) is one of the simplest and most readable versions of Einstein's theory. *Relativity in Illustrations* (New York University Press, 1962), by Jacob Schwartz, illustrates, using completely nontechnical language and lots of pictures and diagrams, the most basic parts of relativity.

In *God and the New Physics* (Simon & Schuster, 1983), theoretical physicist Paul Davies describes the startling discoveries recent physics has made about the nature of time. Steven Hawking's *A Brief History of Time* (Bantam Books, 1988) is a scientifically provocative but historically somewhat inaccurate account by one of the greatest living physicists.

The bizarre and far-reaching revolution in our views of time and space brought about by contemporary relativity theory and quantum mechanics cannot be understood without a grasp of the fundamental mathematical concepts involved; these are explained in *Mathematical Thought* by David Goloff and Daniel Kolak (Paramount/Macmillan, 1996).

CHAPTER 3   WHO

In the West, the philosophical debate over personal identity divides pretty neatly into three phases. The first began with Plato in the fourth century B.C.E. and ended with John Locke in the 1690s. Throughout this period personal identity was explained primarily by appeal to the notion of a spiritual substance, or soul, which was thought to be an immaterial thing. The reflections of Plato that launched this way of understanding the nature of selves, and hence also of personal identity, are in his dialog *Phaedo,* which is about the conversation between Socrates and some of his students on the day that Socrates died.

While others before Plato had talked about the soul as the vehicle for immortality, they had not made it clear that the soul they had in mind was an immaterial thing and not just fine matter. Plato (or Socrates) came closer than anyone before not only to grasping the notion of an *immaterial* thing but also to providing a philosophical rationale for understanding it. In *Phaedo* Socrates speculates about the sources of generation and corruption and suggests that generation involves things coming together and corruption involves their dividing apart. Potentially any compound thing can divide. Implicit in Socrates's discussion is the idea, derived from geometry, that any extended thing is divisible and hence potentially compound. From this it would follow that the only thing we could be sure is incorruptible would be something that is unextended.

Socrates takes it for granted that there are eternal essences of things, which he calls forms, such as the forms of beauty and of equality. Socrates regards these forms as invisible and unchanging. They thus contrast with sensible things, which are visible and constantly in flux. The soul, Socrates argues, is more like the forms than it is like visible things; it makes use of the body to investigate the visible but also withdraws from the body to investigate the forms themselves. The body, Socrates thinks, drags the soul down. When the soul makes use of the body, it acts as if it were drugged or drunk. When it withdraws from the body and contemplates the forms themselves, it is clear-headed. Socrates calls the latter condition *intelligence*.

This discussion in *Phaedo* is the first clear beginning, in the West, of the notion of *dualism*, the thesis that all of reality is divided into two radically different sorts of things: mind and matter. Philosophers who believe that reality consists of just one sort of thing are materialists if they think the basic stuff of reality is matter; idealists if they think it is mind; or neutral monists if they think that reality is some sort of neutral stuff that may be regarded as either matter or mind, depending on how it is understood.

Most Western philosophers from Plato to the seventeenth century were dualists, which fit in well with Christian dogma. However, with the rise of modern science *monism* has gradually replaced dualism. In the seventeenth century Thomas Hobbes argued forcefully for materialism and Spinoza for neutral monism. In the eighteenth century George Berkeley argued for idealism. Arguments among adherents of these different points of view continue to the present day, although now most Western philosophers are materialists, even if they're not as sure as an earlier generation of materialists about what it means to be a materialist. As Jerry Fodor recently put it, "We're all materialists for much the reason that Churchill gave for being a democrat: the alternatives seem even worse" ("The Big Idea," *Times Literary Supplement*, July 1992).

Aristotle, who was Plato's student, was more interested in the soul as a principle of life than as an independently existing, immaterial substance; that is, he was interested in the soul as some aspect of humans and other living things that could explain why they are alive and have the powers that they do. He distinguished among a *vegetative soul*, which is what plants have and which explains why they are alive and can grow; *sensitive soul,* which is what animals have and which explains how they are capable of sense perception, desire, local motion, imagination, and memory; and a *rational soul,* which is what humans have. Although Aristotle was not always consistent in his view about the rational soul, he seems to have thought that it is incorporeal but inseparable from the body in all of its powers except *nous,* or reason.

Aristotle, unlike Plato, did not think it was a bad thing for the soul to be "entombed" in the body. However, he did agree with Plato that *nous* is separable from the body because it preexists the body and is immortal. For Aristotle, the principle of individuation—what distinguishes one thing from another—was matter; therefore, it's not clear how, in his view, there could be more than one soul apart from the body. Aristotle's view of the soul is expressed in several of his writings but primarily in *Eudemus, Protrepticus, On Philosophy, On the Generation of Animals,* and *On the Soul* (all available in many translations and editions).

From John Locke until the late 1960s, major theorists tended to explain personal identity not by the persistence of an immaterial substance but rather in terms of physical and/or psychological relations between a person at different times (say, between you yesterday and you right now). In Locke's view, psychological relations between a person at various times determine whether the "two people" are the same person. The psychological relation that Locke thought matters most is consciousness, by which he is usually understood to mean memory. In this memory interpretation of Locke's view, if you today remember having the experiences and performing the actions that someone had and did yesterday, then you today and that person who existed yesterday are the same person; otherwise, the two of you are not the same person. Locke's views may be found in his *An Essay Concerning Human Understanding,* Book II, chapter 27 (Awnsham & Churchil, 2d ed., 1694; Oxford University Press, 1979). For a selection from Locke and also excerpts from the subsequent historically important literature until 1971, see John Perry, ed., *Personal Identity* (University of California Press, 1975). See also Raymond Martin and John Barresi's "Hazlett on the Future of the Self," *The Journal of the History of Ideas,* v. 56, 1995, pp. 463–81; Raymond Martin, John Barresi, and Alessandro Giovannelli's "Fission Examples in the Eighteenth and Early Nineteenth Century Personal Identity Debate," *History of Philosophy Quarterly,* 1998; and Martin and Barresi's *Naturalization of the Soul: Self and Personal Identity in the Eighteenth Century* (Routledge, 2000). Currently Martin and Barresi are nearing completion of a more general history of self and personal identity theory, tentatively entitled *I, Me, Mine: The Rise and Fall of Soul and Self.*

Since the late 1960s there have been three major developments in Western thought about personal identity. First, *intrinsic* relational views, according to which what determines whether a person at different times is identical is just how the two are physically and/or psychologically related to *each other*, have been largely superseded by *extrinsic* relational (or closest-continuer, or externalist) views. Here what determines whether a person at various times is identical is not just how the two are physically and/or psychologically related to *each other* but also how they are related to *every other* person. So, for instance, in Locke's internalist view, you today are the same person as someone who existed yesterday if you are memory-connected to that person. In an externalist version of Locke's view, one would have to take into account not only whether you are memory-connected to that person of yesterday but also whether anyone else besides you today is memory-connected to that person. One of the best discussions of this aspect of recent theory is the first chapter of Robert Nozick's *Philosophical Explanations* (Harvard University Press, 1981).

Second, the traditional, *metaphysical* debate over personal identity has spawned a closely related but novel debate over egoistic survival *values*—that is, over whether identity or other relations that do not suffice for identity do, or should, matter primarily in a person's egoistic concern to survive. So, for instance, one question might be whether there are any circumstances in which your desire to survive would be better satisfied by your ceasing and being continued by someone who is not you but who embodies many of your most valued characteristics. The most influential discussion of this development occurs in Derek Parfit's "Personal Identity" in *The Philosophical Review*, v. 80, 1971, pp. 3–27, and in Part III of his *Reasons and Persons* (Oxford University Press, 1984). Many philosophers regard *Reasons and Persons* as the most important book on the philosophy of personal identity in the twentieth century.

Finally, since the late 1960s some theorists have replaced the traditional three-dimensional view of people with a four-dimensional view. Roughly speaking, the difference between the two views is that in a three-dimensional view a person can exist at a given moment of time; for instance, you exist right now. In a four-dimensional view, only time-slices or "stages" of people exist at given moments. People exist as aggregates of such person-stages, beginning with the person-stage that came into being at a person's birth, ending with the person-stage that existed when he or she died, and including every person-stage between those two limits. Discussion of the question of which of these two views is theoretically better can get technical quickly; see David Lewis's "Survival and Identity" in

Amélie Rorty, ed., *The Identities of Persons* (University of California, 1976, pp. 17–40); Derek Parfit, "Lewis, Perry, and What Matters," also in Rorty, ed., pp. 91–107; and Lewis's "Postscript to 'Survival and Identity,'" *Philosophical Papers*, v. I (Oxford University Press, 1983, pp. 55–77).

A good elementary discussion of many of these theoretical developments may be found in John Perry's *A Dialogue on Personal Identity and Immortality* (Hackett, 1978) and in James Baillie's *Problems in Personal Identity* (Paragon House, 1993). Daniel Kolak and Raymond Martin, eds., *Self & Identity: Contemporary Philosophical Issues* (Macmillan, 1990), is a comprehensive anthology of current philosophical thought on the problems of unity of consciousness, personal identity, and self. Another good source for the most important recent work is Harold Noonon, ed., *Personal Identity* (Dartmouth Publishing Company, 1993).

The really serious student should also consult the following papers and books: Mark Johnston, "Human Beings," *Journal of Philosophy*, v. 84, 1987, pp. 59–83; John Perry, "Can the Self Divide?" *The Journal of Philosophy*, v. 69, 1972, pp. 463–88; Carol Rovane, "Branching Self-Consciousness," *The Philosophical Review*, v. 99, 1990, pp. 355–95; Sydney Shoemaker, "Persons and Their Pasts," *American Philosophical Quarterly*, v. 7, 1970, pp. 269–85, and "Personal Identity: A Materialist Account," in Sydney Shoemaker and Richard Swinburne, *Personal Identity* (Basil Blackwell, 1984), pp. 69–152; Roy Sorensen, *Thought Experiments* (Oxford University Press, 1992); Ernest Sosa, "Surviving Matters," *Nous*, v. 24, 1990, pp. 305–30; Peter Unger, *Identity, Consciousness, and Value* (Oxford University Press, 1991); Kathleen Wilkes, *Real People* (Oxford University Press, 1988); Stephen White, "Metapsychological Relativism and the Self," *Journal of Philosophy*, v. 86, 1989, pp. 298–323; and Bernard Williams, "The Self and the Future," *The Philosophical Review*, v. 79, 1970, pp. 161–80. Excerpts from most of these sources are included in Kolak and Martin, eds., *Self & Identity*.

On the interesting idea that you don't even have a self, see David Hume's classic statement in Part IV, Book I, of *A Treatise of Human Nature*, first published in 1739 and 1740 (2d ed., Oxford University Press, 1978). Peter Unger takes the idea even further in his "I Do Not Exist" in G. F. MacDonald, ed., *Perception and Identity* (Cornell University Press, 1979, pp. 235–51). Daniel Dennett, in "The Origins of Selves," *Cogito*, 1990 (reprinted in Kolak and Martin, eds., *Self & Identity*), argues that just as novelists invent fictional characters, so the human brain invents the fiction of self.

Thomas Nagel's "Brain Bisection and the Unity of Consciousness" in *Mortal Questions* (Cambridge University Press, 1979) is an intriguing foray into the problems about identity raised by literally mind-splitting neurosurgery. Oliver Sacks's *The Man Who Mistook His Wife for a Hat* (Harper &

Row, 1987) is a wonderfully entertaining and accessible discussion of brain problems that lead to identity problems. In "Personal Identity and Causality: Becoming Unglued," *American Philosophical Quarterly*, v. 24, 1987, pp. 337–47, the authors of the present book argue that much less is essential to our identities over time than either laypersons or philosophers ordinarily assume.

Daniel Kolak's *From Plato to Wittgenstein: The Historical Foundations of Mind* (Wadsworth, 1994) traces the history of ideas leading up to twentieth-century threories of mind. On the value of thought experiments in investigations of personal identity, see Daniel Kolak, "The Metaphysics and Metapsychology of Personal Identity: Why Thought Experiments Matter in Deciding Who We Are," *American Philosophical Quarterly*, v. 30, 1993, pp. 39–53; and on the question of personal identity in connection with multiple personalities, see his "Finding Our Selves: Identification, Identity and Multiple Personality," *Philosophical Psychology*, v. 6, 1994, pp. 363–86, reprinted in Daniel Kolak and Raymond Martin, eds., *The Experience of Philosophy*, 5th ed. (Wadsworth, 2002). Kolak's forthcoming novel, *The Train*, a philosophical journey into questions about personal identity, is currently being developed as a screenplay for a motion picture. His *In Search of Self: Life, Death and Personal Identity* (Wadsworth, 1996) presents in novel form a dramatic encounter among Descartes, the Goddess of Philosophy, and the narrator, exploring the timeless issues of self, personal identity, and the nature of mind and reality. His *Introduction to the Philosophy of Mind* presents an integrated view of developments from the moderns to the present, including the latest research in cognitive science and artificial intelligence.

Raymond Martin has published extensively on questions of personal identity and what matters in survival. His latest views may be found in *Self-Concern: An Experiential Approach to What Matters in Survival* (Cambridge University Press, 1998). An outstanding biological account of human identity may be found in Eric Olson, *The Human Animal* (Oxford University Press, 1997).

Milan Kundera's "The Hitchhiking Game," in *Laughable Loves* (Knopf, 1974) is about a couple who innocently begin playing a game about their identities that gets deeper and deeper, revealing masks beneath masks, until finally they are no longer sure of what the truth is or of who they really are.

Richard Rorty's *Contingency, Irony and Solidarity* (Cambridge University Press, 1989) and Joseph Margolis's *Science Without Unity* (Basil Blackwell, 1987) contain extended discussions of the self from unusually broad perspectives.

Multiple-personality disorder is discussed expertly in Stephen Braude, *First Person Plural: Multiple Personality and the Philosophy of Mind*

(Routledge, 1992). For a thought-provoking historical account, see Ian Hacking, *Rewriting the Soul: Multiple Personality and the Sciences of Memory* (Princeton University Press, 1995). An article that builds a bridge between psychology and philosophy on this issue is Daniel Kolak's "Finding Our Selves: Identification, Identity and Multiple Personality Disorder," in *Philosophical Psychology*, 6 (1993), pp. 363–86.

The notion of self has, of course, also been discussed extensively in Asian philosophical traditions. In Indian philosophy the idea that one's true self is identical with Atman is a recurring theme of the *Vedas, Upanishads, Bhagavad Gita,* and the writings of the six orthodox schools of classical Hindu philosophy. Buddhists deny the existence of the self. In classical Chinese philosophy it was not so much the nature of the self as that of selfless behavior that was of primary concern. One of the best sources of original documents in all of these traditions is J. and P. Koller, eds., *A Sourcebook in Asian Philosophy* (Macmillan, 1991), which includes selections from classical Hindu, Jain, Buddhist, Confucian, and Taoist sources as well as many selections from twentieth-century thinkers. See also William de Bary, *The Buddhist Tradition in India, China, and Japan* (Vintage Books, 1972). One of the least formal of contemporary introductions to Buddhist thought about the self is Sujata, *Beginning to See* (Apple Pie Books, 1983), which includes many marvelous epigrams and cartoons. Phillip Kapleau's *The Three Pillars of Zen* is one of the best introductions, for Americans, to Zen thought and practice. An interesting critique of Asian views may be found in Paul Edward's *Reincarnation: A Critical Examination* (Prometheus Books, 1996). Raymond Martin has edited a selection of Jiddhu Krishnamurti's more philosophical thoughts about self and identity in *Krishnamurti: Reflections on the Self* (Open Court, 1997).

Daniel Kolak explores philosophical issues having to do with personal identity in his novel, *In Search of Myself: Life, Death and Personal Identity* (Wadsworth, 1999), in which the Goddess of Philosophy appears to Descartes in a series of dreams and proceeds to enlighten him. In his *I Am You: The Metaphysical Foundations for Global Ethics* (Kluwer Academic, 2001), Kolak presents his view that there exists but one person, and that we are all that one and the same, numerically identical person.

CHAPTER 4   FREEDOM

Historically there have been three main sources of worry about the possibility of human freedom. The first of these has been that the behavior of all objects in nature is governed by natural law; the second, that everything that happens has been fated to occur; and the third, that there is a God who knows in advance every action that humans will perform. One or another of these has seemed to many to rule out the possibility of human freedom. The first two worries arose in the West in classical Greece and then regained new vigor in the modern period. The third arose in the West in the Middle Ages and, among religious philosophers and theologians, has persisted to the present day.

One of the first Western philosophers to speculate about how humans could be free in a world mostly governed by natural law was Epicurus in the fourth century B.C.E. He accepted Democritus's idea that all objects in nature are composed of atoms. In developing this view Epicurus claimed that only bodies can act and be acted upon and that this can happen only by blows and rebounds, hence, by contact (he had trouble explaining magnetic phenomena's apparent action at a distance). In Epicurus's view people too are simply objects in nature and therefore are composed of atoms. With no creator and no destiny, people come into being and pass away when all of the material conditions for their origin and dissolution have been met. The meeting of these conditions depends ultimately on atomic movements. People's behavior too depends ultimately on atomic movements. Atoms, Epicurus thought, naturally move downward. They can be forced out of their downward path by colliding with other atoms. However, some atoms, in their downward movement, unaccountably swerve. These swerves, which are spontaneous departures from the steely necessity of natural law, create a space for human freedom. For Epicurus's own writings, see W. J. Oates, ed., *The Stoic and Epicurean Philosophers* (Random House, 1940); for an excellent commentary on his views, see C. Bailey, *The Greek Atomists and Epicurus* (Oxford University Press, 1928).

The idea that humans can be free if only their actions are causally undetermined has not been widely accepted in the twentieth century because it has seemed to many that uncaused actions would be random and therefore no more free than caused ones. However, one philosopher to whom the idea has been appealing is William James, in his "The Dilemma of Determinism," *Unitarian Review*, 1884, and in *Essays on Faith and Morals* (Longmans, Green, 1949). For a splendid discussion of the idea that the world is partially undetermined, see Wesley Salmon, *Scientific Explanation and the Causal Structure of the World* (Princeton University Press, 1984).

Returning now to Greek thought, Aristotle (384–322 B.C.E.) neither accepted the atomic theory nor had much to say about the threat to human freedom posed by natural law. He concentrated instead on the problem of explaining how, in the normal course of human life, people distinguish voluntary from involuntary behavior (see his *Nicomachean Ethics*). However, Aristotle did have a metaphysical worry about fate. In a famous passage in his *On Interpretations* he worried about how it could be true today that there will be a sea battle tomorrow unless it were necessary that there be a sea battle tomorrow—that is, unless the sea battle tomorrow were not already somehow "in the cards." Aristotle's answer is obscure. For a contemporary discussion of Aristotle's worry, see Richard Taylor, "Fatalism," *Philosophical Review,* v. 71, 1962, pp. 56–66.

The problem of fatalism that worried Aristotle directly anticipated the medieval worry about how freedom could be possible if God foreknows what will happen. The problem is this: Because God must know in advance every action that every human will perform, including every sin he or she will commit, how could people behave otherwise than God knows they will behave? St. Augustine (354–430 C.E.) answered that even though God foresees everything that is going to occur, things do not occur *because* God foresees them. Augustine claimed that just as someone's remembering an action does not render the action involuntary, so too God's foreseeing it does not render it involuntary. For a lively and much-discussed contemporary statement of the problem of reconciling God's foreknowledge with human freedom, see Nelson Pike's "Divine Omniscience and Voluntary Action," *The Philosophical Review,* v. 74, 1965, pp. 27–46. In "Causality, Responsibility, and the Free Will Defense" in Daniel Kolak and Raymond Martin, eds., *Self, Cosmos, God* (Harcourt Brace Jovanovich, 1993), Daniel Kolak concedes that there is a kind of free will that is compatible with divine foreknowledge, but he claims that it blocks an answer to the problem of evil that would be acceptable to believers in God. Other works on the same theme include Luis de Molina, *On Divine Foreknowledge* (Cornell University Press, 1988); William Hasker, *God, Time, and Knowledge* (Cornell University Press, 1989); and Linda Zagzebski, *The Dilemma of Freedom and Foreknowledge* (Oxford University Press, 1991).

After the rise of modern science, the problem of reconciling human freedom with natural law again assumed center stage. Baron Holbach, in his *System of Nature* (1770), argued famously that no such reconciliation is possible. Today, of course, since it is a tenet of modern science that nature itself includes random events, few philosophers assume that all human actions are causally determined. Instead, like Peter van Inwagen in his well-known and rigorous *An Essay on Free Will* (Oxford University Press, 1983), they often argue that if all human actions were causally determined, then no action would be free. For excellent discussions of van Inwagen's and related arguments, see Michael Slote's "Selective Necessity and the Free-Will Problem," *Journal of Philosophy,* v. 74, 1982, pp. 5–25, and Kadri Vihvelin's "The Modal Argument for Incompatibilism," *Philosophical Studies,* v. 53, 1988, pp. 227–44.

For a newcomer to the issue of human freedom, some of the best discussions are Clarence Darrow's summations to juries, collected in *Attorney
for the Damned*, A. Weinberg, ed. (Simon & Schuster, 1957). This famous
American trial lawyer argued eloquently and (to the juries to whom his
arguments were presented) convincingly that no human actions are free
and therefore no one is responsible for anything he or she does. Others,
such as John Hospers in "Free Will and Psychoanalysis," *Philosophy and
Phenomenological Research*, v. 20, 1950, have drawn on psychoanalytic theory
to make a similar point. A more evenhanded introduction to the issue of
human freedom may be found in chapter 4 of John Hospers's *An Introduction to Philosophical Analysis* (Prentice Hall, 1953).

Among the older but still quite useful anthologies that give a good
sample of all sides of the issue, see Sidney Hook, ed., *Determinism and Freedom in the Age of Modern Science* (Collier Books, 1961); S. Morgenbesser and
J. Walsh, eds., *Free Will* (Prentice Hall, 1962); and Keith Lehrer, ed., *Freedom
and Determinism* (Random House, 1966). Newer, excellent collections of
writings may be found in Ronald C. Hoy and L. Nathan Oaklander, eds.,
Metaphysics (Wadsworth, 1991), and Gary Watson, ed., *Free Will* (Oxford
University Press, 1982), which includes Harry G. Frankfurt's important and
much-discussed "Freedom of the Will and the Concept of a Person," originally published in *Journal of Philosophy*, v. 68, 1971, pp. 5–20.

Since the Enlightenment, Christians, such as Thomas Reid in "The Liberty of Moral Agents," chapters 1 and 9 of *Essays on the Active Powers
of the Human Mind* (1815), and C. A. Campbell in *Of Selfhood and Godhood*
(Macmillan, 1957), have tended to defend free will by appeal to the idea
that people have immaterial souls that are not subject to natural law.

Also since the Enlightenment, many other philosophers have been
drawn to a view often labeled soft determinism, according to which causal
determinism and human freedom are compatible. One of the first and most
influential attempts to defend free will in this way was David Hume's
"Liberty and Necessity" in *An Enquiry Concerning Human Understanding*
(1748). An unusually clear and brief defense of this view may be found in
G. E. Moore's *Ethics* (Oxford University Press, 1912). A contemporary defense of it, with special attention to models of human mentality inspired by
computers and artificial intelligence, may be found in Daniel C. Dennett's
Elbow Room (MIT Press, 1984). Richard Taylor argues forcefully against this
soft-deterministic conception of human freedom in his very accessible
"Freedom and Determinism," *Metaphysics*, 4th ed. (Prentice Hall, 1992),
where he also develops a positive theory of agency that is something like
Reid's view but without the immaterial soul.

Douglas R. Hofstadter's "Who Shoves Whom Around Inside the Careenium? or, What Is the Meaning of the Word 'I'?" in *Metamathematical Themas* (Basic Books, 1985) is a lively and entertaining dialog between Achilles and the Tortoise. On the question of whether addicts have free will, see Kadri Vihvelin's penetrating discussion in "Stop Me Before I Kill Again," pp. 115–48 in the v. 75, 1994, issue of *Philosophical Studies*, which also includes other interesting discussions of free will.

Other generally quite sophisticated discussions that contain valuable insights and arguments are Robert Kane, *Free Will and Values* (State University of New York Press, 1985); Bernard Berofsky, *Freedom from Necessity: The Metaphysical Basis of Responsibility* (Routledge & Kegan Paul, 1987); Alan Donagan, *Choice* (Routledge & Kegan Paul, 1987); Michael Zimmerman, *An Essay on Moral Responsibility* (Rowman & Littlefield, 1988); Susan Wolf's readable *Freedom Within Reason* (Oxford University Press, 1990); and Robert Audi's synoptic *Action, Intention, and Reason* (Cornell University Press, 1993), especially chapters 7 and 10. Eugene Schlossberger, in his *Moral Responsibility and Persons* (Temple University Press, 1992), argues that we are responsible not so much for what we do as for who we are. For a rather offbeat but precise contemporary discussion of freedom and will, see N. M. L. Nathan's *Will and World* (Oxford University Press, 1992). Nathan argues for the Shopenhauerian thesis that will is primary in nature. Recently Saul Smilansky has argued provocatively that we could not live adequately with complete awareness of the truth about human freedom, in *Free Will and Illusion* (Oxford University Press, 2000).

In Indian philosophy the problem of human freedom has been a central concern from the beginning. It became an important concern in Chinese philosophy during the Sui and T'ang dynasties (589–906 C.E.) through the writings of such Buddhist thinkers as Tu-shun, Fa-tsang, Hui-neng, and Shen-hui. For an excellent collection of the classical texts from Indian, Chinese, and a few Japanese sources, see J. and P. Koller, eds., *A Sourcebook in Asian Philosophy* (Macmillan, 1991). For Westerners the best introduction to Chinese philosophy, although not to Chinese Buddhism, is A. C. Graham's *Disputers of the Tao* (Open Court, 1989). Wapola Rahula's *What the Buddha Taught*, 2d ed. (Grove Press, 1978), written by a Buddhist monk, is a highly respected secondary source on Buddhist views. For the views on freedom of two contemporary Tibetan Buddhists, see Chögyam Trungpa's *The Myth of Freedom* (Shambala, 1976) and Tarthang Tulku's *Knowledge of Freedom* (Dharma, 1984). Section 7 of Tulku's book, "Inner Knowledge," is especially useful. Both books use traditional Buddhist concerns about human freedom as a basis for formulating a philosophy of life. For a helpful introduction to the classical literature, see Joel J. Kupperman, *Classic Asian Philosophy: A Guide to the Essential Texts* (Oxford University Press, 2000).

CHAPTER 5 KNOWLEDGE

One of the features distinguishing philosophy from all areas of knowledge is its central concern with the question not merely of *what* you know but *how* you know it. The branch of philosophy dealing with theories of knowledge is called *epistemology*. You can find its beginnings in Plato's *Republic*, where he makes the distinction between knowledge and opinion and formulates the theory of forms and his view that knowledge is merely recollection; the first discussion of the theory of innate ideas is in his *Meno*. Both Platonic dialogues are translated by Benjamin Jowett (Oxford University Press, 1896).

The view that, in varying degrees, nobody knows anything is generally called *skepticism*. The best modern statement of this position can be found in the first two sections of René Descartes's *Meditations on First Philosophy* (Cambridge University Press, 1986), first published in 1640. This work changed the face of modern philosophy by bringing questions about both the nature and extent of human knowledge to the center of philosophical discussion. Without any technical jargon, these dozen or so pages can still pull the rug, and even the floor, right out from under anyone who reads them. Two readable and interesting commentaries on Descartes are Fred Feldman's *A Cartesian Introduction to Philosophy* (McGraw-Hill, 1986) and Harry Frankfurt's *Demons, Dreamers and Madmen* (Bobbs-Merrill, 1970).

The British empiricist and great modern philosopher David Hume further advanced skepticism in his *Treatise of Human Nature* (1739), where he argues that although mathematical and logical knowledge may be possible, empirical and metaphysical knowledge are impossible. For a twentieth-century philosopher's attempt to refute skepticism, see G. E. Moore's famous "A Defense of Common Sense," reprinted in his *Philosophical Papers* (George Allen & Unwin, 1959). In his *Ignorance: A Case for Skepticism* (Oxford University Press, 1975), Peter Unger argues for skepticism.

One of the greatest of all British philosophers, John Locke, in his famous *Essay Concerning Human Understanding* (1690) develops and then critically responds to the views of Descartes. Locke attacks the idea of innate knowledge, argues that all ideas in the mind can be accounted for through experience, and puts forth his representational theory of perception. Another pivotal philosopher and also a British empiricist, George Berkeley, in his groundbreaking *A Treatise Concerning Human Understanding* (1710) puts forth the famous dictum *esse est percipi* ("to be is to be perceived"), pushes the empirical theory of knowledge to its extremes, and develops an idealist theory of knowledge. A different sort of approach to knowledge can be found in the great German philosopher Gottfried Leibniz's *New Essays on the Human Understanding* (1705); for an accessible and rich treatment of all aspects of Leibniz's views, see *Leibniz's New Essays Concerning Human Understanding* (1888) by John Dewey. Dewey is an important philosopher in his own right and one of the founders of the pragmatic theory of knowledge, called *pragmatism*. Immanuel Kant's *Critique of Pure Reason*, trans. Norman Kemp Smith (St. Martin's Press, 1965), widely regarded as one of the major achievements in philosophy, is very difficult. For access to his enormously influential theory about how knowledge is possible, read his *Prolegomena to Any Future Metaphysics* (Open Court, 1902). For an excellent introduction to early twentieth-century epistemology, especially with regard to issues having to do with the philosophy of language, see Bertrand Russell's *Human Knowledge: Its Scope and Limits* (Simon & Schuster, 1948).

A good introduction to the study of knowledge is W. V. O. Quine and J. S. Ullian, *The Web of Belief*, 2d ed. (Random House, 1978). Much of the important twentieth-century work on perception, up to 1964, is well represented in R. J. Swartz, ed., *Perceiving, Sensing and Knowing* (Anchor, 1965). Two more recent anthologies are Roderick Chisholm and Robert Swartz, eds., *Empirical Knowledge: Readings from Contemporary Sources* (Prentice Hall, 1973) and George Pappas and Marshall Swain, eds., *Essays on Knowledge and Justification* (Cornell University Press, 1978). Significant recent developments may be found in Fred Dretske's readable *Seeing and Knowing* (University of Chicago Press, 1969), Dretske's *Knowledge and the Flow of Information* (MIT Press, 1981), Robert Nozick's *Philosophical Explanations* (Harvard University Press, 1981), Keith Lehrer's *Knowledge* (Oxford University Press, 1974), and Peter Unger's *Ignorance* (Oxford University Press, 1975). Raymond Martin has criticized the reliability accounts of knowledge of Dretske and Nozick in "Empirically Conclusive Reasons and Scepticism," *Philosophical Studies*, v. 28, 1975, pp. 215–17, and "Tracking Nozick's Sceptic: A Better Method," *Analysis*, v. 43, 1983, pp. 28–32. Other excellent discussions of knowledge may be found in Robert Fogelin's *Pyrrhonian Reflections on Knowledge and Justification* (Oxford University Press, 1994), Michael Ayers' magisterial *Locke*, 2 vols. (Routledge, 1991), and Keith Lehrer's helpful introduction, *Theory of Knowledge*, 2d ed. (Westview, 2000).

Two useful introductions to the logic of scientific reasoning are Brian Skyrms's *Choice and Chance*, 2d ed. (Dickinson, 1975), and Ronald Giere's *Understanding Scientific Reasoning*, 2d ed. (Holt, Rinehart & Winston, 1984).

W. V. O. Quine's *From a Logical Point of View* (Harvard University Press, 1953) and *Ontological Relativity and Other Essays* (Columbia University Press, 1969) provide excellent examples of a hard-nosed scientific approach by one of the most influential of today's philosophers, whereas Thomas Kuhn's *The Structure of Scientific Revolutions*, 2d ed. (University of Chicago Press, 1970), delivers a mighty blow to the idea that science is objective. Kuhn's book has become one of the most widely discussed philosophy books of the last several decades. Israel Scheffler responds lucidly to Kuhn's arguments in his *Science and Subjectivity*, 2d ed. (Hackett, 1982). Paul Feyerabend mounts the attack against scientific objectivity anew in *Against Method* (Humanities Press, 1975) and in many other stimulating and often beautifully outrageous books and papers.

The problem of knowing things historically and the traditional approaches to solving it are nicely summarized in William Dray's *Philosophy of History*, 2d ed. (Prentice Hall, 1995) and William Dray, ed., *Philosophical Analysis and History* (Harper & Row, 1966). Raymond Martin argues for a new analytical approach to the philosophy of history in *The Past Within Us* (Princeton University Press, 1989) and in *Philosophy of History from the Bottom Up: An American Revolution* (forthcoming). For an excellent selection of postmodernist perspectives on history, see Frank Ankersmit and Hans Kellner, eds., *A New Philosophy of History* (University of Chicago Press, 1995). For a representative sample of the best recent work in philosophy of history, see B. Fay, P. Pomper, and R. Vann, eds., *History and Theory: Contemporary Readings* (Blackwell, 1998).

Gettier's highly influential article "Is Justified True Belief Knowledge?" (*Analysis* 23, 1963, pp. 121–23) in only three pages provides a devastating counterexample to the view that knowledge is justified true belief. Alvin Goldman tries to counter with a causal account of knowledge in his "A Causal Theory of Knowing" (*The Journal of Philosophy*, v. 64, 1967, pp. 355–72) and "Discrimination and Perceptual Knowledge" (*The Journal of Philosophy*, v. 73, 1976, pp. 771–91). Another attempt to repair the hole made by Gettier can be found in Gilbert Harman's *Thought* (Princeton University Press, 1973).

In his *Structure of Empirical Knowledge* (Harvard University Press, 1985) Laurence BonJour criticizes *foundationalism*, the widely held view that knowledge must have a foundation, and argues for a version of *coherentism*, in which justification is achieved not by some fundamental proposition but rather by the way propositions cohere with each other. Alvin Goldman, in "What Is Justified Belief?" (*Justification and Knowledge: New Studies in Epistemology*, George Pappas, ed., D. Reidel, 1979), criticizes all *internalist* theories, which hold, generally, that knowledge depends on states internal to the knower. This can be contrasted with *externalism*, the view that knowledge does not require internal states to which the knower has some special access but, rather, depends on external factors such as some reliable belief-producing mechanism; Goldman thus argues for a type of *reliabilism*. On the opposite end of the spectrum is John Pollock's "Epistemic Norms" (*Synthese*, v. 71, 1987, pp. 61–95), in which he argues for a subjectivist and internalist theory of epistemic justification. For a contemporary theory of knowledge that makes no explicit mention of justification, see Roderick Chisholm's *Perceiving: A Philosophical Study* (Cornell University Press, 1957). For the current debate concerning the shift away from justification altogether and replacing it with *warrant*, see Alvin Plantinga's *Warrant: The Current Debate* (Oxford University Press, 1993). Plantinga puts forth his own theory in *Warrant and Proper Function* (Oxford University Press, 1993). An excellent selection of recent works may be found in Sven Berneker and Fred Dretske, eds., *Knowledge: Readings in Contemporary Epistemology* (Oxford University Press, 2000). On the relationship of knowledge to logic, including game theory, see Daniel Kolak's *On Hintikka* (Wadsworth, 2001).

CHAPTER 6   GOD

Traditional arguments for the existence of God can be found in the following classical works. The *ontological* argument, which attempts to prove the existence of God from the nature of God, can be found in St. Anselm's *Proslogium* (1077). René Descartes also puts forth such an argument in his *Meditations*. For the *cosmological* argument, see the *Basic Writings of St. Thomas Aquinas* (Anton Pegis, ed., Random House, 1945). William Paley's *Natural Theology* (Faulder, 1805) contains the *argument from design*. For an ancient non-Western view of God, see *The Bhagavad Gita*; a good translation is by Franklin Edgerton (Harvard University Press, 1972).

An excellent discussion of mysticism, especially of arguments for the existence of God based on mystical and religious experience, can be found in Rudolf Otto's *Mysticism East and West* (Bracey & Payne, trans., Macmillan, 1932). Three classic Western philosophical accounts sympathetic to faith, religious experience, and mysticism are Søren Kierkegaard's nineteenth-century classic *Concluding Unscientific Postscripts* (Princeton University Press, 1969); William James's *The Varieties of Religious Experience* (Longmans, Green, 1902); and W. T. Stace's provocative *Mysticism and Philosophy* (Lippincott, 1960). Abbott's *Flatland*, mentioned in chapter 1, is also highly relevant as allegory. For an innovative and balanced account of the mystic's claim to have experienced ultimate reality, see Robert Nozick's treatment in *Philosophical Explanations* (Harvard University Press, 1981). An excellent comprehensive anthology is Terence Penelhum, ed., *Faith* (Macmillan, 1989).

The classic discussion of the argument for God based on apparent design in the universe is David Hume's *Dialogues Concerning Natural Religion*, originally published in 1776 and available in many suitable editions. Richard Taylor, in *Metaphysics*, 4th ed. (Prentice Hall, 1993), gives an interesting recent defense of the argument for God based on apparent design in the universe. David Johnson, in *Hume, Holism, and Miracles* (Cornell University Press, 2000), attempts to refute Hume's classic argument against miracles. To see how a top-flight physicist makes room for God in the modern scientific world, see Freeman Dyson's beautifully written *Infinite in All Directions* (Harper &Row, 1988).

For a philosophically sophisticated defense of religious belief, one can do no better than the following: Alvin Plantinga's *God, Freedom and Evil* (Eerdmans, 1977) and *Faith and Rationality* (University of Notre Dame, 1983); Richard Swinburne's *Coherence of Theism* (Oxford University Press, 1977) and *Faith and Reason* (Oxford University Press, 1981); William Alston's *Religious Belief and Philosophical Thought* (Harcourt Brace Jovanovich, 1963); and Garth Hallett's *A Middle Way to God* (Oxford University Press, 2000). In Thomas V. Morris, ed., *God and the Philosophers* (Oxford University Press, 1994) twenty prominent, mostly Christian, philosophers explain the sources of their religious commitments.

One of the most provocative and irreverent attacks ever on belief in God is Bertrand Russell's "Why I Am Not a Christian" in *Why I Am Not a Christian and Other Essays on Religion and Related Topics* (Allen & Unwin, 1957). Ernest Nagel's "A Defense of Atheism," originally in J. E. Fairchild, ed., *Basic Beliefs* (Sheridan House, 1959) and frequently reprinted, is a classic defense of the nonbeliever's position. More lengthy but equally powerful treatments can be found in Michael Scriven's *Primary Philosophy* (McGraw-Hill, 1975), Wallace E. Matson's *The Existence of God* (Cornell University Press, 1965), and J. L. Mackie's *The Miracle of Theism* (Oxford University Press, 1982). J. C. A. Gaskin's *The Varieties of Unbelief* (Macmillan, 1989) is a historically comprehensive anthology of religious skepticism from Epicurus to Sartre. A different sort of attack on religious belief, together with insightful discussions of the possibilities for living without it, can be found in any one of J. Krishnamurti's books, such as his delightfully accessible *Think on These Things* (Harper & Row, 1964) and *Freedom from the Known* (Harper & Row, 1969).

Nelson Pike's *God and Evil* (Prentice Hall, 1964), with its helpful bibliography, is a good place to begin a more careful study of the problem of evil and the various replies to it. An excellent place to begin thinking about the question of free will is Clarence Darrow's summation to the jury in the famous Leopold and Loeb case, one of the most gripping philosophical speeches of all time, published in Arthur Weinberg, ed., *Attorney for the Damned* (Simon & Schuster, 1957). A number of other sources are listed after the "Freedom" chapter above. An unusual and insightful exploration of the importance of free will may be found in Susan Wolf's "The Importance of Free Will," *Mind*, v. 90, 1981, pp. 378–86. And no student should even *think* about leaving the university and going out into the world without reading and pondering Stanley Milgram's *Obedience to Authority* (Harper & Row, 1975).

Daniel Kolak's *In Search of God: The Language and Logic of Belief* (Wadsworth, 1994) explores traditional religious questions from a contemporary philosophical perspective, including the existence of God, the nature of belief, the status of scientific explanations such as quantum genesis, and the role of mystery in our attempts to understand the world. Raymond Martin's *The Elusive Messiah: A Philosophical Overview of the Quest for the Historical Jesus* (Westview, 1999) explains and assesses the challenge posed to Christianity by recent historical scholarship. Those interested in a similar issue in Islam should read Ibn Warraq, *The Quest for the Historical Muhammad* (Prometeus Books, 1999). Daniel Kolak's *The Philosophy of Religion: Classical and Contemporary Issues* (Mayfield 1999) contains classical and the latest, state-of-the-art readings on all the leading topics in the philosophy of religion.

CHAPTER 7   REALITY

The best way to get access to Western thought on the nature of reality is to study the great philosophers, especially Plato's *Phaedo, Republic, Parmenides, Theatetus,* and *Sophist;* Aristotle's *Categories, Posterior Analytics, Physics, De Anima,* and *Metaphysics;* René Descartes's *Meditations, Principles,* and *The World;* G. W. Leibniz's *Monadology;* John Locke's *Essay Concerning Human Understanding;* George Berkeley's *The Principles of Human Knowledge* and *Three Dialogues Between Hylas and Philonous;* David Hume's *Treatise of Human Nature* and *Inquiry Concerning Human Understanding;* and Immanuel Kant's *Critique of Pure Reason.*

Some extremely useful contemporary summaries of the major metaphysical issues include Richard Taylor's *Metaphysics*, 4th ed. (Prentice Hall, 1993), and D. W. Hamlyn's *Metaphysics* (Cambridge University Press, 1984). Readable recent surveys include Bruce Aune's *Metaphysics: The Elements* (University of Minnesota Press, 1985) and W. R. Carter, *The Elements of Metaphysics* (McGraw-Hill, 1990).

Raymond Smullyan, in "Dream or Reality," from *5000 B.C.* (St. Martin's, 1983), Daniel Kolak, in "The Experiment," in *Sirius*, no. 38, 1979, and Robert Nozick, in "Fiction," in *Ploughshares*, Fall 1980, explore one of the oldest themes in history—that reality is a dream.

The important twentieth-century literature tends to be rather technical and would be difficult reading for nonphilosophers. But for those who wish to be up to date on the basic issues and who are willing to make the effort, the following are highly recommended: G. Frege's "Sense and Reference" in P. Geach and M. Black, eds., *Translations from the Philosophical Writings of Gottlob Frege,* 2d ed. (Blackwell, 1970); B. Russell, "On Denoting," *Mind,* v. 14, 1905, pp. 479–93; P. Strawson, "On Referring," *Mind,* v. 59, 1950, pp. 320–44; W. Quine, *From a Logical Point of View* (Harvard University Press, 1953), especially chapters 1, 2, and 8; his "Translation and Meaning" in *Word and Object* (MIT Press, 1960); his "On the Reasons for the Indeterminacy of Translation," *Journal of Philosophy,* v. 67, 1967, pp. 178–83; and his "Ontological Relativity" in Quine, *Ontological Relativity and Other Essays* (Columbia University Press, 1969); H. Grice and P. Strawson, "In Defense of a Dogma," *Philosophical Review,* v. 65, 1956, pp. 141–58; H. Grice, "Meaning," *Philosophical Review,* v. 66, 1957, pp. 377–88; S. Kripke, *Naming and Necessity* (Harvard University Press, 1980), and his *Wittgenstein on Rules and Private Language* (Harvard University Press, 1982); B. Brody, *Identity and Essence* (Princeton University Press, 1980), especially chapters 1–5; David Lewis, "New Work for a Theory of Universals," *Australasian Journal of Philosophy,* v. 61, 1983, pp. 343–77; D. Davidson, "Truth and Meaning," *Synthese,* v. 17, 1967, pp. 304–23; his "True to the Facts," *Journal of Philosophy,* v. 66, 1969, pp. 748–64; and his "Reality without Reference" in M. Platts, ed., *Reference, Truth, and Reality* (Routledge & Kegan Paul, 1980); R. Rorty, "The World Well Lost," *Journal of Philosophy,* v. 69, 1972, pp. 649–65; M. Dummett's "Realism" in *Truth and Other Enigmas* (Harvard University Press, 1978); H. Putnam, *Meaning and the Moral Sciences* (Routledge & Kegan Paul, 1978), especially Parts I and IV; J. L. Mackie, *The Cement of the Universe* (Oxford University Press, 1974), especially chapters 2, 3, and 7; and Terence Parsons, *Nonexistent Objects* (Yale University Press, 1980).

Many of the preceding views are extremely well explained, and then criticized, in Michael Devitt's *Realism and Truth,* 2d ed. (Princeton University Press, 1997). For excellent discussions of the nature of reality, see Milton Munitz's *Cosmic Understanding* (Princeton University Press, 1990), and *The Question of Reality* (Princeton University Press, 1990). Daniel Kolak's *From the Presocratics to the Present* (Mayfield, 1998) presents a history of the philosophical developments in the evolution of the human concept of reality, from the ancients to the present.

CHAPTER 8   EXPERIENCE

The most important foundational discussions of the nature of experience, in particular the issues of whether we directly experience the world, the distinction between percepts and concepts, and the representational nature of perception, can be found in the classic works of Descartes, Locke,

Berkeley, Hume, Leibniz, and Kant, already mentioned. There is no better link between these classical views and twentieth-century developments than William James's "Does 'Consciousness' Exist," *Journal of Philosophy, Psychology and Scientific Methods*, v. 1, no. 18, 1904; "A World of Pure Experience," *JPPSM*, v. 1, nos. 20 and 21, 1904; and "Percept and Concept" in *Some Problems of Philosophy*, chapters 4 and 5 (Longmans, Green, 1911), all of which are reprinted in Daniel Kolak's *From Plato to Wittgenstein: The Historical Foundations of Mind* (Wadsworth, 1994).

The relationship between consciousness and physiology has been much discussed by twentieth-century philosophers. Three classic treatments are L. Wittgenstein's *Philosophical Investigations* (Blackwell, 1953), Gilbert Ryle's *Concept of Mind* (Hutchinson, 1949), and W. Sellers's "Empiricism and the Philosophy of Mind" in *Science, Perception, and Reality* (Routledge & Kegan Paul, 1971). Until the 1970s the main issue was whether conscious states can be identified with brain states. Two excellent anthologies that represent the best thought on this issue are D. Rosenthal, ed., *Materialism and the Mind-Body Problem* (Prentice Hall, 1971) and J. O'Connor, ed., *Modern Materialism: Readings on Mind-Body Identity* (Harcourt, Brace & World, 1969). Daniel Dennett's "Current Issues in the Philosophy of Mind," *American Philosophical Quarterly*, v. 15, 1978, pp. 249–61, an excellent source for students, is a clear and accessible account of how and why this main traditional issue became transformed in more recent debates.

Dennett and Hofstadter's *The Mind's I* (Basic Books, 1981) and Paul Churchland's *Matter and Consciousness*, rev. ed. (MIT Press, 1988), are also good places to begin the study of the relation between mind and brain. Also important are Daniel Dennett's *Brainstorms* (Bradford, 1978); J. Fodor's *The Language of Thought* (Harvard University Press, 1979), *Representations* (MIT Press, 1981), as well as his *Modularity of Mind* (MIT Press, 1983); and N. Block, "Troubles with Functionalism," *Minnesota Studies in the Philosophy of Science*, v. 9, 1978, pp. 261–325. Thomas Nagel's by now classic "What Is It Like to Be a Bat?" *Philosophical Review*, October 1974, reprinted in Kolak and Martin, eds., *The Experience of Philosophy*, 4th ed. (Wadsworth, 1999), and Nagel's more recent *The View from Nowhere* (Oxford University Press, 1986) are intriguing attempts to state the antireductionist view that there is more to consciousness than what can be captured in our current scientific theories. See also Valerie Hardcastle, *The Myth of Pain* (MIT Press, 2000).

Two excellent experiential accounts that deconstruct interpretation and thought from immediate experience are D. E. Harding, *On Having No Head* (Harper & Row, 1972), an excerpt of which appears in *The Experience of Phi-*

losophy, and Jean-Paul Sartre's philosophical novel *Nausea* (New Directions, 1964). Both dramatize the power and catharsis of confronting one's experience of the world directly rather than through theory.

CHAPTER 9 CONSCIOUSNESS

Emile Meyerson's classic *Identity and Reality* (Dover, 1962), originally published in 1906, is a sophisticated yet accessible account of scientific explanation that raises the interesting question of where reductionism might lead. The novelist and philosopher Arthur Koestler is probably the best-known critic of reductionism. His *Janus: A Summing Up* (Vintage, 1979) is one of his best; along with J. R. Smithies, he published the anthology *Beyond Reductionism* (Beacon Press, 1983). For a criticism of Koestler's approach, see Stephen Toulmin's amusing essay on Koestler in *The Return to Cosmology* (University of California Press, 1982).

Two recent philosophical contributions to the reductionism debate are Frank Jackson, "Epiphenomenal Qualia," *Philosophical Quarterly,* v. 32, 1982, pp. 127–136, and Paul Churchland, "Reduction, Qualia, and the Direct Introspection of Brain States," *Journal of Philosophy,* v. 82, 1985, pp. 8–28, both included in Daniel Kolak and Raymond Martin, eds., *The Experience of Philosophy,* 5th ed. (Wadsworth, 2002). An excellent computational account of consciousness may be found in Peter Carruthers's *Language, Thought, and Consciousness* (Cambridge University Press, 1998).

On the relationship between mind and nature, John Gribbin's *In Search of Schrödinger's Cat* (Bantam, 1984) is great fun. On this topic the works of Werner Heisenberg, Erwin Schrödinger, John Archibald Wheeler, and Paul Davies listed in the next chapter are all appropriate.

For some of the latest developments, see John Searle's "Is the Brain's Mind a Computer Program?" (*Scientific American,* Jan. 1990) and David Chalmers, *The Conscious Mind* (Oxford University Press, 1996). A recent popular book is *The Emperor's New Mind: Concerning Computers, Minds and the Laws of Physics* by Roger Penrose (Oxford University Press, 1989), which is usefully contrasted with the also popular book by Daniel Dennett, *Consciousness Explained* (Little, Brown, 1991).

A good source for important work on consciousness, from the 1960s and '70s, is vol. 2 of Ned Block, *Readings in the Philosophy of Psychology* (Harvard University Press, 1981). More recent work may be found in three comprehensive anthologies: William G. Lycan, ed., *Mind and Cognition* (Basil Blackwell, 1990); Alvin I. Goldman, ed., *Readings in Philosophy and Cognitive Science* (MIT Press, 1993); and Robert and Denise Cummins, eds., *Minds, Brains, and Computers: The Foundation of Cognitive Science* (Blackwell,

2000)—these latter anthologies contain selections from the most influential, recent work of Noam Chomsky, Jerry Fodor, Hilary Putnam, Stephen Stich, Paul Churchland, Patricia Churchland, Fred Dretske, Daniel Dennett, Janet Levin, Andy Clark, John Searle, Georges Rey, William Lycan, John Hauge-land, Kim Sterelny, Keith Campbell, and Hartry Field. Daniel Kolak's *The Philosophy of Mind* (Mayfield, 1999) contains a selection of leading classical readings in the philosophy of mind. For an excellent assessment of many of these issues, see Georges Rey, *Contemporary Philosophy of Mind* (Blackwell, 1996).

CHAPTER 10 COSMOS

As we have seen, one answer to the question of where the universe came from is that it arose spontaneously, from nothing. Philosophers and mystics have always been preoccupied with the concept of nothingness. As Peter Heath remarked in "Nothing," v. 5 of *The Encyclopedia of Philosophy* (Macmillan, 1967), ever since the pre-Socratic Greek philosopher (and mys-tic) Parmenides "laid it down that it is impossible to speak of what is not, broke his own rule in the act of stating it, and deduced himself into a world where all that ever happened was nothing [Parmenides thought that mo-tion and change are impossible], the impression has persisted that the nar-row path between sense and nonsense on this subject is a difficult one to tread and that altogether the less said of it the better."

It is hard for philosophers to avoid the notion of nothingness. It looms in the background, stalking philosophical theories. Plato, for instance, who was profoundly influenced by Parmenides, thought that anything about which one can have knowledge must exist as a constant and abiding referent of one's talk about that thing. In other words, he thought that if one has knowledge of something, say, of some geometrical truth, then there must be something stable of which one has this knowledge. Since the sensible world of material objects is in constant flux—that is, is constantly and rapidly passing from being into nothing—one can't, Plato claimed, have stable and abiding knowledge of sense objects. Hence, he concluded, there is an ideal world of super-sensible forms—Beauty, Justice, Equality, and so on—that can be understood not through the senses but only through thought. This world of forms, he reasoned, is the object of our knowledge. See especially Plato's *Timaeus, Parmenides,* and *Republic.*

For scientists too the notion of nothingness has been important, even before the advent of modern science. For instance, the medieval scientific dictum *ex nihilo nihil fit* (out of nothing nothing comes) is the presupposi-tion that lies behind the conservation laws of matter and energy in classical physics. Since the advent of quantum mechanics in the 1920s, the dictum has become suspect but in a way that enhances the importance of the notion of nothingness. As Isaac Asimov explains these developments, in 1973 the American physicist Edward P. Tryon showed that "it was possible for a Universe to appear, as a tiny object, out of *nothing*. Ordinarily, such a Universe would quickly disappear again, but there were circumstances under which it might not." Asimov explains, "In 1982 Alexander Vilenkin combined Tryon's notion with the inflationary Universe and showed that the Universe, after it appeared, would inflate, gaining enormous energies at the expense of the original gravitational field, and would not disappear. However," he continues, the Universe "would eventually slow its expansion, come to a halt, begin to contract and return to its original tiny size and enormous temperature, and then, in a 'Big Crunch,' disappear into the nothingness from which it came." This quotation appears in *Beginnings* (Berkeley Books, 1987).

In *God and the New Physics* (Simon & Schuster, 1983) the physicist Paul Davies explains the same remarkable theoretical developments by noting that "recent discoveries in particle physics have suggested mechanisms whereby matter can be created in empty space by the cosmic gravitational field, which only leaves the origin of spacetime itself as a mystery. But even here there are some indications that space and time could have sprung into existence spontaneously without violating the laws of physics." According to Davies, "In this remarkable scenario the entire cosmos simply comes out of nowhere, completely in accordance with the laws of quantum physics, and creates along the way all the matter and energy needed to build the universe we now see. It thus incorporates the creation of all physical things, including space and time. Rather than postulate an unknowable singularity to start the universe off, the quantum spacetime model attempts to explain everything entirely within the context of the laws of physics." Davies concludes, "It is an awesome claim. We are used to the idea of 'putting something in and getting something out,' but getting something for nothing (or out of nothing) is alien. Yet the world of quantum physics routinely produces something for nothing. Quantum gravity suggests we might get everything for nothing." Finally, the physicist Alan Guth has remarked, "It is often said that there is no such thing as a free lunch. The universe, however, is a free lunch."

A good introduction to the view that consciousness is necessary for the universe to exist is G. Gale's "The Anthropic Principle," *Scientific American*, v. 254, Dec. 1981, pp. 154–71. The most comprehensive book on the Anthropic Principle is J. Barrow and F. Tippler's *Anthropic Cosmological Principle* (Oxford University Press, 1986). Parts of it are technical; in particular, some of the mathematical physics might be inaccessible, but this drawback should not prevent anyone from understanding the full sweep of the powerful and rich new ideas expressed in it about the relationship between ourselves and the cosmos. John Archibald Wheeler's *Mind in Nature* (Harper & Row, 1982) is also important. See, also, Daniel Kolak's "Quantum Cosmology, the Anthropic Principle, and Why Is There Something Rather Than Nothing?" in *The Experience of Philosophy*, 5th ed. (Wadsworth, 2002).

For those who would like to approach the subject with some background, Erwin Schrödinger's *Mind & Matter* (University Press, 1958) is an excellent beginning, as is his beautifully written and utterly accessible little book *What Is Life?* (Cambridge University Press, 1967). Additional easy access to modern physics is Werner Heisenberg's *Physics and Philosophy* (Harper & Row, 1962) and *Physics and Beyond* (Harper & Row, 1971). Heisenberg, famous for his Uncertainty Principle, is candid and personal about how he arrived at some of his views; particularly revealing is his account of how, after ruminating on Plato's *Timaeus*, he came to the conclusion that the ultimate constituents of everything must be not physical but mathematical.

Paul Davies, one of the best expositors of physics for the nonspecialist, wrote several books that have chapters on the Anthropic Principle. His *God and the New Physics* (Touchstone, 1984), *Edge of Infinity: Where the Universe Came From and How It Will End* (Simon & Schuster, 1981), and *Other Worlds* (Simon & Schuster, 1980), are free of equations and provide superb introductions into the mind-boggling world of quantum physics. For those who want math, his *Quantum Mechanics* (Routledge & Kegan Paul, 1984) is superb, as is his *The Accidental Universe* (Cambridge University Press, 1982).

The notion of nothingness looms large in Martin Heidegger's philosophy. Heidegger, a pre–World War II phenomenologist, heavily influenced the development of existentialism after the war. Heidegger's first and most important book, *Sein und Zeit* (1927; trans. into English as *Being and Time*, Harper & Row, 1962), is divided into two parts. In the first, he describes what he takes to be our inauthentic existence. Human beings, he claims, have three essential and interrelated traits: facticity, existentiality, and forfeiture (or fallenness). *Facticity* means that humans always find themselves already in a world; that is, they find themselves already contextualized. Your world could no more be the world it is without you than you could be you without it. One aspect of our fundamental state, then, according to Heidegger, is "being-in-the-world." *Existentiality* means the way in which humans appropriate their world, making it their own. We exist, Heidegger thinks, in a constant state of anticipation of our own possibilities. We are always reaching out beyond ourselves. Our very being consists in aiming at *what does not yet exist*. *Forfeiture* means that in our everyday mode of living we are constantly distracted by our lives with others and for others in a way that makes us forget the central task of becoming ourselves.

In the second part of *Being and Time* Heidegger explains what he takes to be authentic existence. His response to the question whether there is any emergence from forfeiture, or fallenness, is that the answer lies in looking at the moods that characterize the momentary states of the individual. One of these moods is *Angst,* or dread. And dread, according to Heidegger, uniquely has the power to recall humans from self-betrayal to self-knowledge. Whereas other moods and passions focus on everyday objects in the world, dread has no such nameable, isolated object but instead focuses on the loss of objects, that is, on nothingness.

To acquire such an authentic focus on nothingness, Heidegger claims, one must attend not to this or that thing or person but to one's whole structure of being-in-the-world, for this structure is bounded by nothingness. In other words, in Heidegger's view, to confront your life, which is your world, authentically, you must confront it in its entirety, and to confront it in its entirety, you must confront the end of your world, which is your death. Such a confrontation with death, or nothingness, Heidegger claims, is the path not only to authenticity but also to freedom. Authentic human being, he says, is "being-to-death." In "Martin Heidegger" in v. 3 of *The Encyclopedia of Philosophy* (Macmillan, 1967), Marjorie Green sums up this central aspect of Heidegger's view as follows: "If human being is to be a unity, it can be so only as a whole, that is, in relation to its ending, death. If human being is to rise from forfeiture to authenticity, it can do so only in isolation from the seductive 'they.' Only death, or the relation to death, brings such isolation, for my death is the only event in my life, Heidegger says, which is uniquely mine: It is *eigentlich* ('authentic') because it is *eigen* ('my own')."

Heidegger's much later work, *An Introduction to Metaphysics* (1953; trans. into English, Anchor Books, 1961), is entirely devoted to the question "Why is there something rather than nothing?" It is sometimes penetrating but often only marginally intelligible; for instance, in it Heidegger tries to find Being in a schoolhouse but finds instead only chalk.

In Milan Kundera's novel *The Unbearable Lightness of Being* (Harper & Row, 1984), which was heavily influenced by Heidegger's philosophy, the author evokes the idea that Being is so insubstantial as to be almost, but not quite, nothing. Jean-Paul Sartre, who as a young man was a student of Heidegger's, was also profoundly affected by Heidegger's views on nothingness. This influence shows up especially in Sartre's early novel *Nausea* (1938; trans. New Directions, 1949) and in his magnum opus, *Being and*

Nothingness (1943; trans. Philosophical Library, 1956). Sartre's deepest interest is in understanding individual human existence. Humans, he thinks, have an aspiration that runs so deeply in them as to be almost definitive of what it is to be human. This aspiration, which Sartre thinks is doomed to failure, is to overcome the contingency of one's own existence and ground it instead in a rational necessity of some sort.

The idea of nothingness, or nonbeing, enters most fully into Sartre's deliberations in connection with his attempt to explain consciousness. Sartre's main clue in providing this explanation is the ability humans have to ask questions and receive negative answers. This is possible, he thinks, because nonbeing is a feature of the world. Sartre criticizes Heidegger for having failed to show how nothingness can be present in a particularized or local form within the world. This is possible, Sartre claims, only if there is a being that generates its own nothingness. Human consciousness, he thinks, is such a being. Its distinguishing feature is to contrast itself with its physical environment, including its body and even its own past. By such self-detaching activity, consciousness creates a hole in the world (really, in "being-in-itself"). Consciousness, Sartre says, is free because it is apart from the world. At the heart of inauthentic human existence is the attempt humans make to conceive of themselves as just another object in the world. Authentic human existence consists in the realization of one's essential detachment from being an object and from any natural causal process. In other words, authentic human existence consists in the realization of one's own freedom. Sartre calls such an experiential realization of one's own freedom the feeling of anguish.

In "The Problem of Being," chapter 3 of *Some Problems of Philosophy* (Longmans, Green, 1911), William James argues that the problem of why anything at all exists is fundamental and inescapable. In confronting this issue, James claims, either you have to assume a big unknown all at once, or you must assume a bunch of little unknowns piecemeal. For a prominent contemporary analytic philosopher's views on "explaining everything" and on mystical experience, including the experience of nothingness, see chapter 2 of Robert Nozick's fascinating and instructive *Philosophical Explanations* (Harvard University Press, 1981). Within analytic philosophy more generally the attempt to understand nonbeing often focuses on how negative judgments can be true. Sometimes the attempt takes the form of trying to understand the status of fictional objects. Although the discussion of such issues within analytic philosophy has often been technical, interested readers can get access to the central concerns by considering such classics as Rudolf Carnap's "The Elimination of Metaphysics" in A. J. Ayer, ed., *Logi-*

cal Positivism (Macmillan, 1959) and Bertrand Russell's "On Denoting" in *Mind*, N.S., v. 14, 1905, pp. 479–93. Also of interest are A. N. Prior's "Nonentities" in R. J. Butler, ed., *Analytical Philosophy* I (Oxford University Press, 1962); Richard Taylor's "Negative Things," *Journal of Philosophy*, v. 49, 1952, pp. 433–48; Eric Toms's *Being, Negation and Logic* (Oxford University Press, 1962); and David and Stephanie Lewis's "Holes," *Australasian Journal of Philosophy*, v. 48, 1970, pp. 206–12.

Such ideas, and others, are connected to scientific explanations of the origin of the cosmos in Milton Munitz's *Cosmic Understanding* (Princeton University Press, 1990) and *The Question of Reality* (Princeton University Press, 1990). Good selections of papers on this same topic may be found in James E. Huchinson, ed., *Religion and the Natural Sciences* (Harcourt Brace Jovanovich, 1993) and John Leslie, ed., *Physical Cosmology and Philosophy* (Macmillan, 1990). The latter includes Edward Tryon's 1973 *Nature* paper, "Is the Universe a Vacuum Fluctuation?" For a discussion of the latest developments in quantum cosmology, see Daniel Kolak's "Quantum Cosmology, The Anthropic Principle, and Why Is There Something Rather Than Nothing," in Kolak and Martin, eds., *The Experience of Philosophy*, 5th ed. (Wadsworth, 2002).

CHAPTER 11   DEATH

Plato believed that our lives are only a reflection of another, more perfect world to which we ascend when we die and from which we return back to this world. He invented and perfected the idea of an immaterial soul. *Phaedo* is the best place to start exploring his thoughts on death; for a good selection of the relevant passages see Daniel Kolak and Raymond Martin, eds., *The Experience of Philosophy*, 4th ed. (Wadsworth, 1999) or Paul Edwards, ed., *Immortality* (Macmillan, 1992).

Epicurus, a contemporary of Plato, said in his *Letter to Menoeceus*, "So death, the most terrifying of ills, is nothing to us, since so long as we exist, death is not with us; but when death comes, then we do not exist." These remarks are probably the most discussed statement ever on the significance of death. Contemporary theorists often begin by distinguishing their views from those of Epicurus. One of the best such accounts is Fred Feldman's *Confrontations with the Reaper* (Oxford University Press, 1992). Feldman's book, perhaps the clearest ever written about the nature and significance of death, ends with his thesis that death is bad when it deprives the person who dies of intrinsically valuable experiences.

St. Thomas Aquinas's views on death, which subsequently became official dogma of the Catholic Church, may be found in his two great treatises

Summa Theologica and *Summa Contra Gentiles*. His discussion, an extraordinarily subtle integration of the views of Plato and Aristotle with the tenets of Christian faith, ends with the not-so-subtle observation that once your bodily death occurs, your soul is "either plunged into hell or soars to heaven, unless it be held back by some debt [such as an unforgiven 'venial sin'], for which its flight must needs be delayed until the soul is first of all cleansed." Aquinas says that "this truth is attested by the manifest authority of the canonical Scriptures and the doctrine of the holy Fathers: wherefore the contrary must be judged heretical."

In the 1760s Voltaire wrote a number of "Homilies" in which he advocated deism as a better view than either Christianity or atheism. Although he believed in God, he regarded the possibility that we might survive our bodily deaths as absurd and incredible and *the idea* of death as sad even though *death itself* is "nothing at all." "To cease to love and be lovable," he wrote, "is a death unbearable: to cease to live is nothing." A nice selection of his views may be found in chapter 10 of Paul Edwards, ed., *Immortality* (Macmillan, 1992), which also contains many other excellent selections. Another good anthology is John Donnelly, ed., *Language, Metaphysics, and Death*, 2d ed. (Fordham University Press, 1994).

A critical survey of the major philosophical positions may be found in A. Flew's "Immortality" in v. 4, pp. 139–50, of *The Encyclopedia of Philosophy* (Macmillan, 1967). Surveys of views about reincarnation may be found in Ninian Smart's article in v. 7, pp. 122–25, of the same work and in J. Bruce Lone's article on reincarnation in v. 12, pp. 265–69, of the *Encyclopedia of Religion* (Macmillan, 1967). Ian Stevenson, a psychiatrist at the University of Virginia, in his *Twenty Cases Suggestive of Reincarnation*, 2d ed. (University of Virginia, 1974), provides meticulously researched and fascinating evidence of children who apparently remember their past lives. Raymond Martin, in "Survival of Death: A Question of Values," in *Religious Studies*, v. 28, 1992, and reprinted in Kolak and Martin, eds., *The Experience of Philosophy*, uses one of Stevenson's most dramatic examples to make the point that there may be no fact of the matter about whether we survive our bodily deaths. An excellent, general survey of the evidence for survival of bodily death may be found in Robert Almeder's *Death and Personal Survival* (Littlefield Adams, 1992). A. Gauld, in *Mediumship and Survival* (Granada, 1982), surveys from a psychologist's point of view the evidence for survival. And *Death and Immortality in the Religions of the World*, edited by P. and L. Badham (Macmillan, 1987), contains essays expounding just what its title suggests.

Among contemporary philosophical treatments of the meaning of death for life, Martin Heidegger's *Being and Time* (English trans., Blackwell,

1967) is a difficult read but one that can be thoroughly mesmerizing. Heidegger manages to peel away the framework of commonsense beliefs in the context of which many of us view ourselves and the world, and he challenges readers not only to understand his own alternative view but to actually have their experience change as a consequence of that understanding. Thomas Nagel's "Birth, Death and the Meaning of Life," chapter 11 in *The View from Nowhere* (Oxford University Press, 1986), is in some ways an analytic philosopher's version of Heidegger's view. Sartre's views may be found in his *Being and Nothingness* (Philosophical Library, 1956, pp. 531–53). A good systematic account of existentialist views from Heidegger to Sartre, particularly on the effect that fear of dying has on human life, is Michael Slote's "Existentialism and the Fear of Dying," *American Philosophical Quarterly*, v. 12, 1975, pp. 17–28.

An excellent literary but explicitly nonexistentialist approach to death is explored by Jules Romains in his novel *The Death of a Nobody* (H. Fertig, 1976). Particularly interesting is Romains's development of a social concept of a person. For a literary exploration of the absurdity of death, see Daniel Kolak's "The Wine Is in the Glass" in Kolak and Martin, eds., *The Experience of Philosophy*. One puzzle about death is why the prospect that it is imminent so often challenges the meaning of our lives. After all, what does the fact that our lives will end have to do with whether they are worth living? In "A Fast Car and a Good Woman," Kolak and Martin, eds., *The Experience of Philosophy*, Raymond Martin gives his answer.

A contemporary response to Epicurus that links the discussion of the significance of death to the question of why people take such different attitudes toward the past and the future may be found in Robert Nozick's *Philosophical Explanations* (Harvard University Press, 1981). Derek Parfit illustrates the same question with the following example: "I am an exile from some country, where I have left my widowed mother. Though I am deeply concerned about her, I very seldom get news. I have known for some time that she is fatally ill and cannot live long. I am now told something new. My mother's illness has become very painful in a way that drugs cannot relieve. For the next few months, before she dies, she faces a terrible ordeal. That she will soon die I already knew. But I am deeply distressed to learn of the suffering that she must endure. A day later I am told that I had been partly misinformed. The facts were right but not the timing. My mother did have many months of suffering, but she is now dead" (*Reasons and Persons*, Oxford University Press, 1984, p. 213). Parfit notes that most people, if they were in the place of the person being given this information, would be greatly relieved to learn that their mother had died. He argues that the new piece of information—that one's mother's suffering is in the past—should not have a crucial impact on how one feels about it.

Bertrand Russell's views on just about anything are always worth consulting. His views on death may be found in "The Art of Growing Old" in his *Portraits from Memory and Other Essays* (Simon & Schuster, 1956) and in "What I Believe," in his *Why I Am Not a Christian* (Simon & Schuster, 1957). Freud's views are expressed in "Thoughts for the Times on War and Death" in James Strachey and Anna Freud, eds., *Standard Edition of the Complete Psychological Works of Sigmund Freud*, v. 14 (Hogarth Press, 1957), pp. 288–317.

A good sample of writings on death by contemporary Western philosophers may be found in John Martin Fischer, ed., *The Metaphysics of Death* (Stanford University Press, 1993). Fischer's anthology includes Bernard Williams's well-known "The Makropulos Case: Reflections on the Tedium of Immortality," in which Williams argues that death gives meaning to life and that immortality would be tedious. Another good selection of recent articles can be found in S. T. Davis, ed., *Death and the Afterlife* (St. Martin's Press, 1989). On issues at the intersection of death and ethics, see F. M. Camm, *Morality, Mortality* (Oxford University Press, 1993).

A crucial difference among those who believe that humans survive their bodily deaths is between those who believe in personal survival and those who believe that humans do not survive as individuals but rather are absorbed in some sort of Universal Mind or Soul. Most Christians and most Jews who believe in survival believe in personal survival. But there have been notable exceptions, such as various Christian mystics and some of the New England transcendentalists. The early twentieth-century philosopher/psychologist William James writes with sympathy and respect about Universal Mind as "the mother sea" and "the great reservoir of consciousness." The physicist Erwin Schrödinger and the novelist Arthur Koestler have endorsed a similar view.

In traditional African thought the dead are often thought to be still present and part of one's extended social world even though they are not visible. So, for instance, one can have conversations with one's dead relatives and appeal to them for help. See Kwasi Wiredu's "Religion from an African Perspective" in Daniel Kolak and Raymond Martin, eds., *Self, Cosmos, God* (Harcourt Brace Jovanovich, 1993) and *The Experience of Philosophy* (Wadsworth, 1999).

Classical Asian philosophical texts often combine both the personal and the impersonal versions of the belief in survival. For instance, in Hindu scripture it is written that after many incarnations individual minds are eventually absorbed into Brahman. Some Buddhists have a similar view but substitute Nirvana, which is sometimes conceptualized as a kind of World Consciousness, for Brahman. In classical Chinese philosophy the dominant concerns are more practical than speculative. For instance, while the question of whether "the dead have knowledge" is raised, it tends to be more in terms of whether ghosts can harm the living than of whether people are immortal. The Confucian Hsün-tzu takes it for granted that consciousness ends at death. The Mohists argue at length that the dead are conscious. Otherwise the issue tends to be left open. The Taoist Chuang-tzu is preoccupied with death, but it is with the question of how to reconcile oneself to the fact of death. He sees liberation from selfhood as a kind of triumph over death, a way of grasping that one shall remain what one has always been—not a separate self but rather identical with all the endlessly transforming phenomena of the universe. Many of the classic texts may be found in J. and P. Koller, eds., *A Sourcebook in Asian Philosophy* (Macmillan, 1991). For the views of a contemporary Buddhist who has worked extensively with the dying, see Stephen Levine's *A Gradual Awakening* (Doubleday, 1979) and *Healing into Life and Death* (Doubleday, 1987).

CHAPTER 12   MEANING

For responses by Gandhi, H. L. Mencken, Bertrand Russell, George Bernard Shaw, and many famous others to the ambiguous question of whether life is meaningful, see Will Durant, ed., *On the Meaning of Life* (R. Long & R. R. Smith, 1932). For more substantial selections from a variety of classical and contemporary sources, two of the best current anthologies are E. D. Klemke, ed., *The Meaning of Life,* 2d ed. (Oxford University Press, 1999) and Steven Sanders and David Cheney, eds., *The Meaning of Life* (Prentice Hall, 1980). One of the best attempts to sort out the many ambiguities in the murky but useful expression "the meaning of life" is Kurt Baier's marvelously clear *The Meaning of Life* (Canberra University College, 1957), in which he concludes that, in general at least, there is no basis for pessimism.

One of the most moving of those darker accounts of the meaning of life in which a philosopher *has* found a basis for pessimism is Arthur Schopenhauer's *The World as Will and Idea* (K. Paul, Trench, Traubner, 1886), in which he declares that it is absurd to speak of life as a gift, as so many have done, because "it is evident that everyone would have declined such a gift if he could have seen it and tested it beforehand." Another eloquent account of the apparent pointlessness of life is by the great American trial lawyer and humanist Clarence Darrow, who wrote in *Is Life Worth Living?*

(Girard, Kansas, undated) that "life is like a ship on the sea, tossed by every wave and by every wind . . . headed for no port and no harbor, with no rudder, no compass, no pilot; simply floating for a time, then lost in the waves." In "A Free Man's Worship," *Mysticism and Logic* (Simon & Schuster, 1929), Bertrand Russell found a potent source for pessimissim by looking at what he took to be the long-term prospects of the universe: "All the labors of the ages, all the devotion, all the inspiration, all the noonday brightness of human genius, are destined to extinction in the vast death of the solar system and the whole temple of man's achievement must inevitably be buried beneath the debris of a universe in ruins."

Leo Tolstoy's *Confessions* (Dent, 1905) is a brilliantly written and moving account of a great writer's religious crisis, which he experienced at the height of his fame at the age of fifty. Tolstoy explains how he sought the meaning of life and found it in faith. His discovery led him to advocate humility, nonviolence, vegetarianism, the moral value of manual labor, the avoidance of luxury, and sexual abstinence.

Albert Camus, who won the Nobel Prize for literature, popularized one of the most potent metaphors for the meaninglessness of life: the image of a man, Sisyphus, endlessly pushing a rock up a hill only to have it roll back down again as soon as he reaches the top. Camus explains in *The Myth of Sisyphus and Other Essays* (Knopf, 1955) how by integrity and defiance Sisyphus can live an ennobling life nonetheless. Camus concludes with the optimistic observation, "One must imagine Sisyphus happy." Camus's philosophical novel on the same theme, *The Stranger* (Random House, 1946), is written in such a lucid and engaging style that many find the hero's despair downright uplifting. Also of interest is his novel *The Plague* (Random House, 1948). Jean-Paul Sartre, in his novel *Nausea* (New Directions, 1959), explores similar existentialist themes but in a more pessimistic vein, as he does also in his play *The Flies* (Random House, 1956). For a clear and concise statement of what existentialism is, there is nothing better than Sartre's essay "Existentialism and Human Emotions" (Philosophical Library, 1957). For Sartre's gloomy account of why all human relationships, particularly romantic ones, are doomed to frustrating failure, see his *Being and Nothingness* (Philosophical Library, 1956), Part 3, chapter 3.

Charlotte Perkins Gilman's "The Yellow Wallpaper" is a powerful and haunting story, written in the 1890s, about a sensitive woman who goes mad for lack of meaningful work and an environment in which she can find her own identity. This story can be found in Ann Lane, ed., *The Charlotte Perkins Gilman Reader* (Pantheon, 1980).

The mystical and brooding Ludwig Wittgenstein, one of the founding fathers of twentieth-century analytic philosophy, expresses his views on the meaning of life in his *Notebooks, 1914–1916* (Harper & Row, 1961), pp. 72–83, and in Daniel Kolak's new translation, *Wittgenstein's Tractatus* (Mayfield, 1998).

Richard Taylor's "Does Life Have a Meaning?" in his *Good and Evil* (Prometheus, 1984) and Thomas Nagel's "Birth, Death and the Meaning of Life," chapter 11 in *The View from Nowhere* (Oxford University Press, 1986), are well-known reflections on the meaning of life by contemporary analytic philosophers. Raymond Martin, in "A Fast Car and a Good Woman," critiques the views of Tolstoy, Taylor, and Nagel and ends by questioning the psychological validity of philosophical worries about the meaning of life. Martin suggests that, as often as not, such worries merely mask a deep, underlying problem: our inability to stay satisfied. Martin's article is in Daniel Kolak and Raymond Martin, eds., *The Experience of Philosophy*, 5th ed. (Wadsworth, 2002), which also contains the essays by Tolstoy, Camus, and Taylor already mentioned. See also Alexander Nehamas's award-winning *The Art of Living* (University of California Press, 1998).

For those interested in accounts by psychologists, Victor Frankl's *Man's Search for Meaning* (Beacon, 1963) and Carl Jung's *Man in Search of a Soul* (Harcourt Brace Jovanovich, 1955) are two of the best. *Man's Search for Himself* (Norton, 1953) is by Rollo May, a psychologist who was a disciple of the philosopher Martin Heidegger.

It is possible to organize an entire philosophy of life around the theme of being released from addiction. One of the best efforts of this sort, which has been extraordinarily successful in a practical way, is *Twelve Steps and Twelve Traditions* (Alcoholics Anonymous World Services, 1952). For a Buddhist perspective on recovering from addiction, see Ruth Fishel's *The Journey Within* (Health Communications, 1987).

Lao-tzu's *The Way of Life* is the Taoist classic on how to live well; the Witter Bynner translation (Perigee Books, 1944, 1972) is very good. But for the best and most piercing interpretation and translation, see *On Lao Tzu* by David Cheng (Wadsworth, 2000), which has the additional merit that it replaces the "mystical" with a more properly scientific outlook of the great Chinese sage. For a Zen perspective, Philip Kapleau's *The Three Pillars of Zen* (Anchor, 1980) is an excellent place to start, particularly for anyone who would appreciate sampling one form of meditation. Other highly regarded Buddhist books on the meaning of life include Charlotte Joco Beck's *Everyday Zen* (Harper & Row, 1989); Joseph Goldstein's *The Experience of Insight* (Shambala, 1976); Joseph Goldstein and Jack Kornfield's *Seeking the Heart of Wisdom* (Shambala, 1987); Jack Kornfield's *A Path with a Heart* (Bantam Books, 1993); Shunryu Suzuki's *Zen Mind, Beginner's Mind* (Weatherhill, 1970); and Thich Nhat Hanh's *The Miracle of Mindfulness* (Beacon Press, 1975).

For a penetrating account by a meditative philosopher who rejects all religious traditions, including Buddhism, as well as all conceptions of spiritual practice, see any of the books by Jiddu Krishnamurti. *The Awakening of Intelligence* (Harper & Row, 1976), *Think on These Things* (Harper & Row, 1964), and *Freedom from the Known* (Harper & Row, 1969) are among his best. If you would like to see an unusual synthesis of meditative and scientific approaches, see Krishnamurti's dialogues with the physicist David Bohm in *The Ending of Time* (Harper & Row, 1985).

CHAPTER 13   ETHICS

Historically, the dispositions to believe and to obey authority came first and are by far stronger than the disposition to question. Even today, in what probably is the most skeptical and antiauthoritarian global culture in the history of Earth, there is an astonishingly strong disposition to do what we are told to do by people in positions of authority. For evidence of this, see Stanley Milgram's *Obedience to Authority* (Harper and Row, 1974), a selection from which is reprinted in Daniel Kolak and Raymond Martin's *The Experience of Philosophy*, 4th ed. (Wadsworth, 1999). The art of questioning authority, which has not come easily to humans and which has had to be learned, is a relatively recent invention.

In Asia the art of questioning moral authority began in the sixth century B.C.E. with such figures as Buddha, Lao-tzu, and Confucius. For instance, in a famous passage from the earliest Buddhist scriptures, the Buddha admonishes his students not to follow: "Do not accept what you hear by report, do not accept tradition, do not accept a statement because it is found in our books, nor because it is in accord with your belief, nor because it is the saying of your teacher. . . . Be ye lamps unto yourselves. . . . Those who, either now or after I am dead, shall rely upon themselves only and not look for assistance to anyone beside themselves, it is they who shall reach the very topmost height." For a good selection of the original texts, see J. and P. Koller, eds., *A Sourcebook in Asian Philosophy* (Macmillan, 1991).

In the West the art of questioning moral authority began in Greece in the fifth century B.C.E. with a small group of philosophers, of whom Socrates is the best-known and most accomplished example. For a fascinating and scholarly account of their story, see Gregory Vlastos's *Plato's Universe* (University of Washington Press, 1975). Collectively, these early philosophers launched not only natural science but also the discipline of philosophical ethics, which on its negative side is simply critical reflection on traditional ways of life and rules of conduct and on its positive side is an attempt to formulate better alternatives.

Philosophy, whether in Asia or in the West, arises from the attempt to understand and answer questions of ultimate concern: Who am I? Where do I—and where does everything else—ultimately come from? What, if anything, is the meaning of my life? What will be my fate? What will be the ultimate fate of everything? How, if at all, can I find out what is true? How should I live?

All of these questions, except for the one about meaning and the question of how one should live, have to do exclusively with how things *are* and therefore are the concern of science or metaphysics. The question about meaning and the question of how one should live have to do with how things *should be*—the concern of philosophical ethics.

Initial answers to all of these questions tend to be handed down by religious and cultural authorities. They may tell you, for instance, that God created the cosmos and you, that you have an immortal soul, that this soul will be the vehicle for your personal survival of bodily death, and that to go to heaven you must belong to one church and live by its dictates or subscribe to certain religious and moral beliefs rather than, say, belong to another church or suspend belief until you can discover for yourself what is true.

Soon enough, though, each of us arrives at what must be one of life's most momentous insights: the realization that what we have been taught to believe by our authorities differs dramatically from what others have been taught to believe by their authorities and also, perhaps, from what humans have learned scientifically about the world and its origins.

How you respond individually to this insight makes a great difference to how you lead your life. How we respond collectively may make a great difference to our collective fate as well—perhaps even to whether there will be a future for human life on this planet. Will we dig in our heels and assume that the answers conveyed to us by our authorities are superior to the answers conveyed to others by their authorities—a response that historically has been the typical one and has led to narrowness, intolerance, and war—or will we use our awareness of our differences to rethink our most fundamental commitments? That is the decisive question.

Plato's *Euthyphro* is the classic discussion of religious belief as a source of moral authority. Good contemporary discussions of the same issue may be found in Antony Flew's *God and Philosophy* (Dell, 1966), Kai Nielsen's *Ethics Without God* (Prometheus Books, 1973), Richard Garner's *Beyond Morality* (Temple University Press, 1994), pp. 210–19, and chapter 4, "Does Morality Depend on Religion?" of James Rachels's *The Elements of Moral Philosophy*, 2d ed. (McGraw-Hill, 1993), which also contains one of the best concise introductions to philosophical problems of ethics.

Perhaps the fiercest attack ever on Christian morality was mounted by the nineteenth-century philosopher Friedrich Nietzsche, who declared, "I regard Christianity as the most fatal and seductive lie that has ever yet existed—as the greatest and most *impious* lie," and urged everyone "to declare open war with it." For a good translation and selection of Nietzsche's writings, see either of Walter Kaufman's two anthologies, *The Portable Nietzsche* (Viking, 1954) or *Basic Writings of Nietzsche* (Modern Library, 1967).

So-called divine-command morality, which had been out of favor among professional philosophers for the last 150 years, has made something of a comeback in the last decade among a group of highly talented Christian philosophers. Although their writings tend to be technical, several valuable selections may be found in Gene Outka and John Reeder, Jr., eds., *Religion and Morality* (Anchor, 1973) and Paul Helm, ed., *Divine Commands and Morality* (Oxford University Press, 1981). Richard Swinburne's recent *Responsibility and Atonement* (Oxford University Press, 1989) is a distinguished Christian philosopher's exploration of the religious and moral meaning of merit and guilt. *Aquinas and Natural Law* (Macmillan, 1968), by D. J. O'Connor, is a good introductory account of the philosophical basis for Roman Catholic moral theory.

On the connection between egoism and ethics, see Socrates's response to the example of "Gyges's ring" in Plato's *Republic* (any edition will do) and the writings of the eighteenth-century British moralists Thomas Hobbes and Joseph Butler. Hobbes defends psychological egoism, the view that we have no choice but to pursue our own self-interest, in his *Leviathan* (Blackwell, 1946) and in *On Human Nature* (available in Thomas Hobbes's *Body, Man, and Citizen*, Richard S. Peters, ed. [Collier, 1962]). Butler attacks and, according to many philosophers, decisively refutes psychological egoism in his "Fifteen Sermons Preached at Rolls Chapel," in *Works,* W. E. Gladstone, ed. (Oxford University Press, 1910). Contemporary and very accessible discussions of egoism include Harry Browne's "The Morality Trap" in his *How I Found Freedom in an Unfree World* (Macmillan, 1973); Ayn Rand's *The Virtue of Selfishness* (New American Library, 1964); Joel Feinberg's "Psychological Egoism," in his *Reason and Responsibility* (Wadsworth, 1985); Robert Olson's *The Morality of Self-Interest* (Harcourt, Brace & World, 1965); Michael Slote's "An Empirical Basis for Psychological Egoism" in *Journal of Philosophy,* v. 61, 1964, pp. 530–37; and David Gauthier, ed., *Morality and Rational Self-Interest* (Prentice Hall, 1970).

Richard B. Brandt's "The Use of Authority in Ethics" in his *Ethical Theory* (Prentice Hall, 1959) is excellent. On conscience as a source of moral authority, see Jonathan Bennett's delightfully disturbing essay, "The Conscience of Huckleberry Finn," in *Philosophy,* v. 49, 1974, in which he compares the attitudes of Huckleberry Finn, the Nazi Heinrich Himmler, and the fanatical and sadistic Calvinist theologian and American religious philosopher Jonathan Edwards.

Selections from the essays mentioned by Plato, Bennett, and Nietzsche; historically important selections by Immanuel Kant and John Stuart Mill; and Bertrand Russell's classic defense of ethical subjectivism, "Science and Ethics," are included in Kolak and Martin, eds., *The Experience of Philosophy*.

Ethical relativism and the question of why anyone should be moral is discussed by Louis P. Pojman in his *Ethics: Discovering Right and Wrong* (Wadsworth, 1990). Excellent on the topic of ethical subjectivism is Bernard Williams's sophisticated but readable *Ethics and the Limits of Philosophy* (Harvard University Press, 1985), especially chapter 1, "Socrates's Question," chapter 5, "Styles of Ethical Theory," and chapter 9, "Relativism and Reflection." An up-to-date collection of essays on moral relevatism may be found in P. K. Moser and T. Carson, eds., *Moral Relativism: A Reader* (Oxford University Press, 2000).

A superb overview of philosophical problems of authority can be found in Richard T. DeGeorge's *The Nature and Limits of Authority* (University Press of Kansas, 1985), which also includes an extremely helpful bibliographic essay.

One of the best in the older generation of general anthologies on ethics is Paul Taylor, ed., *Problems of Moral Philosophy* (Wadsworth, 1978). Richard Brandt's *Value and Obligation* (Harcourt, Brace & World, 1961), John Hospers's *Human Conduct* (Harcourt, Brace & World, 1961), and William Frankena's concise *Ethics* (Prentice Hall, 1963), though somewhat dated, are still valuable introductory texts. All four have been used so widely that there is a good chance you can find them in a university library.

Excellent more recent anthologies include Louis Pojman, ed., *Ethical Theory* (Wadsworth, 1989) and Jonathan Glover, ed., *Utilitarianism and Its Critics* (Macmillan, 1990). For a nonutilitarian approach, see Bernard Gert's *Morality: A New Justification of the Moral Rules* (Oxford University Press, 1988).

Applied ethics has been a growth industry for the last two decades, and many good anthologies and texts are now available. Joan Callahan's excellently edited collection, *Ethical Issues in Professional Life* (Oxford University Press, 1988), is one of the best. Other good sources include Richard M. Fox and Joseph P. DeMarco, eds., *Moral Reasoning: A Philosophical Approach to Applied Ethics* (Holt, Rinehart & Winston, 1989); W. Michael Hoffman and Jennifer M. Moore, eds., *Business Ethics* (McGraw-Hill, 1990); Holmes Rolston III, *Environmental Ethics* (Temple University Press, 1990); Pablo Iannone, ed., *Contemporary Moral Controversies in Technology* (Oxford

University Press, 1987); and, on ethical problems in journalism, Anthony Serafini, ed., *Ethics and Social Concern* (Paragon House, 1990).

So-called virtue ethics is the latest trend in ethical theory. Important recent books in this area include Philippa Foot's *Virtues and Vices and Other Essays in Moral Philosophy* (University of California Press, 1978) and James Wallace's *Virtues and Vices* (Cornell University Press, 1978). Alasdair Mac-Intyre's *After Virtue* (University of Notre Dame Press, 1981) is one of the most discussed current treatments of the subject. MacIntyre develops his view in *Whose Justice? Which Rationality?* (University of Notre Dame Press, 1988). A helpful overview of work on the subject through 1984 may be found in Gregory E. Pence's "Recent Work on the Virtues," *American Philosophical Quarterly,* v. 21, 1984, pp. 281–97. Also useful is Pence's article "Virtue Theory" in Peter Singer, ed., *A Companion to Ethics* (Basil Blackwell, 1991), pp. 249–58.

Finally, Richard Garner in *Beyond Morality* (Temple, 1994) argues provocatively that "morality and religion have failed because they are based on duplicity and fantasy" and that the time has come to leave both of them behind and focus our efforts instead on developing compassion. Chapters 5 and 6 of his book contain an informal and easily accessible introduction, aimed at Americans, to the classical moral theories of India and China. See also Roy Perrett's excellent *Hindu Ethics* (University of Hawaii Press, 1998).

CHAPTER 14   VALUES

Many distinctions among kinds of value, or forms of goodness, have been proposed. For instance, the value of a thing may mean its worth or, alternatively, what makes it good (or bad). Well-known typologies of value have been proposed in *An Analysis of Knowledge and Valuation* (Open Court, 1946) by C. I. Lewis, who makes a fivefold distinction, and by G. H. Von Wright in *The Varieties of Goodness* (Routledge & Kegan Paul, 1963).

Probably the most useful distinction philosophers have made in regard to value is that between *instrumental value*—that is, the value that something has in virtue of being a means to something else—and *intrinsic value,* or the value that something has as an end in itself. For instance, for most people (misers excluded) money is valuable only instrumentally as a means to something else, whereas happiness is valuable as an end in itself. Among important philosophers, only John Dewey has explicitly rejected this distinction in his *Theory of Valuation* (University of Chicago, 1939).

For those who accept the distinction between instrumental and intrinsic value, a crucial question arises: What is intrinsically valuable? Among philosophers, the most popular answer has been "pleasure" or "satisfaction." More precisely, many philosophers have claimed that only experiences are intrinsically good and that what makes an experience intrinsically good is the pleasure or satisfaction that it brings to the person (or sentient creature) that has the experience. The view that pleasure and only pleasure is intrinsically good is called *hedonism*. The list of philosophers who have advocated hedonism includes Epicurus, David Hume, Jeremy Bentham, John Stuart Mill, Henry Sidgwick, C. I. Lewis, and with some qualifications Brand Blanshard, whose *Reason and Goodness* (Allen & Unwin, 1966) is an especially clear and accessible discussion of the issue.

In Aristotle's view the one and only thing that is intrinsically good is not pleasure but rather *eudaemonia*, or excellent activity; see his *Nicomachean Ethics* in Richard McKeon, ed., *The Basic Works of Aristotle* (Random House, 1941). Augustine and Aquinas held that the one and only intrinsic good is communion with God; Spinoza, knowledge; F. H. Bradley, self-realization; and Nietzsche, power. For a valuable and nicely written development of Aristotle's views by an important contemporary classicist, see Martha Nussbaum's "Non-Relative Virtues: An Aristotelian Approach" in P. A. French et al., eds., *Midwest Studies in Philosophy, Vol. XII: Character and Virtue* (University of Notre Dame Press, 1988), pp. 32–53. For a more general discussion of value in its relation to virtue by an influential Roman Catholic philosopher, see Peter Geach, *The Virtues* (Cambridge University Press, 1977). Also excellent on the topic of virtue is E. L. Pincoffs's *Quandaries and Virtues: Against Reductionism in Ethics* (University of Kansas Press, 1986).

Other philosophers—so-called pluralists—have held that there is more than one thing that is intrinsically valuable. Plato, G. E. Moore, W. D. Ross, and R. B. Perry, among others, have been pluralists. Among the things they have claimed are intrinsically valuable, in addition to pleasure, are knowledge, beauty, truth, love, friendship, justice, and freedom. They have claimed that some or all of these things are good in and of themselves, not just because they tend to promote pleasure. G. E. Moore, for instance, claimed that it would be better for the world to be beautiful than ugly even if no one ever experienced its beauty; see his *Principia Ethica* (Cambridge University Press, 1903).

Another topic of intense philosophical interest has been the distinction between fact and value and the closely related question of whether value judgments can be objective. David Hume proposes a subjectivist view of values in Book III of *A Treatise of Human Nature* (originally published in 1738 but now available in numerous editions) and in Section I and Appendix I of his *An Inquiry Concerning the Principles of Morals* (1752; available in numerous editions). G. E. Moore gives a classic refutation of what he calls "simple subjectivism" in chapter 3 of his *Ethics* (Oxford University Press, 1912). C. L. Stevenson discusses Moore's argument and advances his own "emotivist" theory of subjective value in *Facts and Values* (Yale, 1963). J. L. Mackie's *Ethics: Inventing Right and Wrong* (Penguin, 1977) is a highly respected and more recent defense of subjectivism by an important analytic philosopher.

For a balanced discussion of both sides of the issue of objectivity in ethics and values, James Rachels's discussion in *The Elements of Moral Philosophy*, 3d ed. (McGraw-Hill, 1999), is quite useful. Also valuable are the relevant sections of Louis Pojman, ed., *Ethical Theory* (Wadsworth, 1989); Jonathan Glover, ed., *Utilitarianism and Its Critics* (Macmillan, 1990); and Bernard Gert's *Morality: A New Justification of the Moral Rules* (Oxford University Press, 1988).

Jean-Paul Sartre's *Existentialism* (Philosophical Library, 1957) is a classic existentialist defense of subjectivism. Sartre's views are sympathetically criticized and then creatively developed by Charles Taylor in "Responsibility for Self" in Amélie O. Rorty, ed., *The Identities of Persons* (University of California Press, 1976). Taylor continues to develop his view in his *Sources of the Self* (Harvard University Press, 1990). Mary Midgley, in *Wisdom, Information & Wonder* (Routledge, 1989), has some interesting criticisms of existentialist theories of value as well as a powerfully expressed alternative view of her own. Mackie's views are criticized by David O. Brink in "Moral Realism and the Skeptical Arguments from Disagreement and Queerness," *Australasian Journal of Philosophy*, v. 62, 1984.

For a view that influenced and in some ways parallels the themes we develop in the present chapter, and also for an American ethicist's perspective on Asian theories of value, see Richard Garner's provocative *Beyond Morality* (Temple University Press, 1993).

On the idea that we can get out from under our current frameworks of values and get a worthwhile perspective on them meditatively, that is, by just watching our thoughts and behavior, see Sujata's charming little book of epigrams and cartoons, *Beginning to See* (Apple Pie Books, 1983); Joseph Goldstein's manual for insight-meditation, *The Experience of Insight* (Unity Press, 1976); and Shunryu Suzuki's classic *Zen Mind, Beginner's Mind* (Weatherhill, 1970).

Self-deception is expertly discussed in Herbert Fingarette's readable *Self-Deception* (Humanities Press, 1969); Mary Haight's *A Study of Self-Deception* (Humanities Press, 1980); Mark W. Martin's two anthologies, *Self-Deception and Self-Understanding: New Essays in Philosophy and Psychology*

(University of Kansas Press, 1985) and *Self-Deception and Morality* (University of Kansas Press, 1986); and Brian McLaughlin and Amélie O. Rorty, eds., *Perspectives on Self-Deception* (University of California, 1988).

Peter Singer's *Practical Ethics* (Cambridge University Press, 1979) provides easy access to the lively contemporary debate over the value of human life, particularly in connection with the issue of abortion. Many of the best papers written on the philosophy of abortion are collected in Joel Feinberg, ed., *The Problem of Abortion*, 2d ed. (Wadsworth, 1984). Michael Tooley's *Abortion and Infanticide* (Oxford University Press, 1983) is somewhat technical but an important study of the question. See also the relevant essays in Tom Regen, ed., *Matters of Life and Death*, 3d ed. (McGraw-Hill, 1993). On the value of animal life, see Peter Singer's groundbreaking *Animal Liberation* (New York Review Books, 1975) and the relevant articles by Singer and others in Regen's *Matters of Life and Death*. Regen's *The Case for Animal Rights* (University of California Press, 1983) is a spirited defense of animal rights by a philosopher/activist. R. G. Frey's *Rights, Killing, and Suffering: Moral Vegetarianism and Applied Ethics* (Blackwell, 1983) ably presents the case for the other side.

Interesting feminist perspectives on values may be found in Simone de Beauvoir's *The Second Sex* (Penguin, 1976); Simone Weil's "Friendship" in *Waiting for God* (Harper & Row, 1983); Adrienne Rich, "Women and Honor: Some Notes on Lying," in her *On Lies, Secrets, and Silence, Selected Prose 1966–1978* (W. W. Norton, 1979); Kate Millet, *Sexual Politics* (Doubleday, 1970); Joan Roberts, ed., *Beyond Intellectual Sexism: A New Woman, A New Reality* (David McKay, 1976); Joan Kelley, *Women, History, and Theory* (University of Chicago Press, 1984); and Marilyn Pearsall, *Women and Values* (Wadsworth, 1986).

The impact of recent and possible technology on values is engagingly discussed by Jonathan Glover in *What Sort of People Should There Be?* (Penguin, 1984). Bertrand Russell's "The Value of Philosophy" in his *Problems of Philosophy* (Oxford University Press, 1912) is a classic. On the nature and practice of philosophy and what it means, see Daniel Kolak's *Lovers of Wisdom*, 2d ed. (Wadsworth, 2001).

Name Index

A

Abbott, E. A., 115, 132
Almeder, Robert, 144
Alston, William, 133
Ankersmit, F., 131
Anselm, St., 132
Aquinas, St. Thomas, 133, 143–144
Aristotle, 117, 119–120, 125–126, 134, 144, 155
Asimov, Isaac, 139
Audi, Robert, 128
Augustine, St., 117, 126, 155
Aune, Bruce, 134
Ayer, A. J., 142
Ayers, M., 130

B

Badham, L., 144
Badham, P., 144
Bailey, C., 125
Baillie, James, 122
Barresi, John, 121–122
Beck, Charlotte Joco, 149
Bentham, Jeremy, 151
Bergson, Henri, 117
Berkeley, George, 119, 129, 134–135
Berneker, Sven, 132
Berofsky, Bernard, 128
Black, Max, 135
Block, Ned, 136–137
Boeke, Kees, 116
Bohm, David, 117, 150
Bonjour, Laurence, 131
Brandt, Richard, 152
Braude, Stephen, 123
Brink, David O., 156
Brody, B., 135
Browne, Harry, 151
Buddha (Sidhartha Gotama), 149

C

Cajori, Florian, 117
Callahan, Joan, 153
Camm, F. M., 146
Campbell, C. A., 127
Campbell, Keith, 138
Camus, Albert, 148
Carnap, Rudolf, 142
Carruthers, Peter, 137
Carson, Thomas, 153
Carter, W. R., 134
Chalmers, D., 137
Cheng, David, 149
Chisholm, Roderick, 130, 132
Chomsky, Noam, 138
Churchill, Sir Winston, 119
Churchland, Patricia, 138
Churchland, Paul, 137–138
Clark, Andy, 138
Confucius, 150
Cummins, Denise, 137
Cummins, Robert, 137

D

Danzig, Tobias, 116
Darrow, Clarence, 127, 133, 147
Davidson, D., 135
Davies, Paul, 118, 139–140
De Bary, 124
De Beauvoir, Simone, 157
DeGeorge, Richard T., 153
DeMarco, J. P., 153
Democritus, 125
Dennett, Daniel C., 116, 122, 127, 136–138
Descartes, René, 129, 132, 134–135
Devitt, Michael, 135
Dewey, John, 130, 154
Donagan, Alan, 128